Praise for *Boy, Lost*

'A powerful memoir. Olsson's prose is lyrical and heartfelt.' ***Books + Publishing***

'[An] engrossing, affecting family memoir.' ***Weekend Australian***

'A compelling story of a family torn apart by poverty and abuse, evocatively told by a gifted writer.' ***Courier-Mail***

'An intelligent and deeply serious book about lives full of pain.' ***Australian Book Review***

'A shatteringly beautiful read, one not easily forgotten. I can't recommend it highly enough.' ***The Newtown Review of Books***

'The writing is beautiful and Olsson's ability to capture a person or a moment is stunning – but it's the fierceness and restraint she demonstrates in this memoir that makes it so moving.' ***The Conversation***

'Olsson uses perfectly balanced prose and enormous compassion to weave breathtaking beauty into this family memoir. Highly recommended.' ***Readings Monthly***

'A harrowing yet beautifully written tale.' ***Good Reading***

'Exquisitely written and achingly intimate, this is a significant book which sets a new benchmark for memoir.' **Judges' comments, Queensland Literary Awards**

'A compassionate and sensitive entwined narrative of a lost son and lost mother, this book – by virtue of Olsson's writing – soars above the conventions of its genre.' **Judges' comments, Victorian Premier's Literary Awards**

'Much of the power of this book lies in the way that it reflects the fates of all children lost to a parent or parents, and that lifts it beyond the level of merely personal memoir to give it some of the force of fable and folktale.' **Judges' comments, Stella Prize**

Kristina Olsson is the author of the novel *In One Skin* (2001) and the biography *Kilroy Was Here* (2005). Her second novel, *The China Garden* (2009), received the 2010 Barbara Jefferis Award for its empowering depiction of women in society and was also shortlisted for the Kibble Literary Award. Kristina's non-fiction work *Boy, Lost: A Family Memoir* won the 2013 Queensland Literary Award, the New South Wales Premier's Literary Award, the Western Australian Premier's Literary Award, and the Kibble Literary Award. It has been shortlisted for the Victorian Premier's Literary Award, Stella Prize, Australian Human Rights Commission Literature Award and *The Courier-Mail* Book of the Year People's Choice Award. Kristina's journalism and non-fiction have been published in the *Australian,* the *Courier-Mail,* the *Sunday Telegraph* and *Griffith REVIEW.* She has worked extensively as a teacher of creative writing and journalism at tertiary level and in the community, and as an advisor to government. She lives in Brisbane. Her latest novel is *Shell.*

Boy, Lost

KRISTINA OLSSON

UQP

First published 2013 by University of Queensland Press
PO Box 6042, St Lucia, Queensland 4067 Australia

This edition published 2023

University of Queensland Press (UQP) acknowledges the Traditional Owners and
their custodianship of the lands on which UQP operates. We pay our respects to their
Ancestors and their descendants, who continue cultural and spiritual connections to
Country. We recognise their valuable contributions to Australian and global society.

uqp.com.au
reception@uqp.com.au

Cover design by Christabella Designs
Cover photograph by Shutterstock
Typeset in Bembo by Post Pre-press Group, Brisbane
Printed in Australia by McPherson's Printing Group

 **Queensland** University of Queensland Press is supported by the
Government Queensland Government through Arts Queensland.

  University of Queensland Press is assisted
by the Australian Government through
the Australia Council, its arts funding
and advisory body.

Parts of the Author's Note appeared as an essay in *Good Weekend*, December 2019.

A catalogue record for this book is available from the National Library of Australia.

ISBN 978 0 7022 26605 8 (pbk)
ISBN 978 0 7022 26708 6 (epdf)
ISBN 978 0 7022 26711 6 (epub)

University of Queensland Press uses papers that are natural, renewable and recyclable
products made from wood grown in well-managed forests and other controlled
sources. The logging and manufacturing processes conform to the environmental
regulations of the country of origin.

For my mother and Peter
For my father and Sharon
For Lennart, Ashley and Andrew

Cairns railway station, far north Queensland, summer, 1950. A girl with fugitive eyes and an infant on her hip. She is thin, gaunt even, but still it is easy to see these two are a pair, dark-haired and dark-eyed. She hurries down the platform towards the second-class cars, slowed by the weight of her son and her cardboard suitcase. It holds everything they own, everything she dared to take.

She finds a seat in one of the last cars – perhaps it feels safe, perhaps she is already getting as far from this place as she can – and settles herself. She has some food wrapped in paper, a dry sandwich, arrowroot biscuits – there was nothing else in the flat. Peter – that is the boy's name – is tired, fractious, out of routine. Somewhere in her own weary brain she knows he is echoing her, responding to her own fear, her own curdled mix of terror and sorrow and the adrenalin it has taken to get her here. She talks to him quietly, she hopes he won't cry. She doesn't want anyone to hear him.

This is the scene as I see it, sixty years later. It is sepia-toned, like the photographs I have of her then. Nineteen years old, with a face people compared to the young Elizabeth Taylor, and fine-boned limbs. But the fineness apparent through her thin shift that day had nothing to do with her natural build. She was malnourished, starving. Later, when she stumbles off the train in Brisbane she will be taken away to hospital. No one will know until then – no one could tell – that the new pregnancy she'd protected and kept secret was now well advanced.

But that is days later. Whole days and a lifetime from the minutes she waited on the train, willing it to move, to take them to safety. A lifetime because surely that is how long the journey seemed, how long she'll have, later, to recall over and over a single moment. The man appears at the door of the carriage, walks towards her – a twisted smile – and roughly pulls Peter from her arms. Later, in memory and dream and conversation, she will wonder what else he said to her, apart from those few chilling words. *Don't move* – the Greek accent was heavy and cruel; the baby whimpered, reached for his mother, a biscuit in his fist – *Don't move, you bitch. Stay on the train or you're dead. Him too.* She knew from the brutality of the past months that he meant it.

He waited then, his bulk blocking the doorway, until a whistle blew and the train shuddered. Did she plead with him in those minutes, beg, tell him she'd stay? Did she try to strike a bargain, some pathetic deal? I doubt it. In the parlance of the poker games he was addicted to, she had nothing to bargain with, no cards to play. She had only herself, her own bruised and flimsy body, her poor bullied heart. He didn't want *her*.

This is the story my mother never told, not to us, the children who would grow up around it in the way that skin grows over a scratch. So we conjured it, guessed it from glances, from echoes, from phrases that snap in the air like a bird's wing, and are gone. Fragments of a legend, that's how it seemed, and it twisted through our childhood like a fiction we had read and half-forgotten; a story that belonged to others, not to us, and to another, long-ago time. As if the woman at its centre was not really our mother but a stranger, an unknowable version of her, not the woman who made our school lunches, plastered our cuts, grimaced daily over the washing tub and wringer. Smiled as we came in the door.

We knew questions were off-limits. The story had its own force-field, our mother's sadness as effective as any electric fence. So we learned to live alongside it, or rather, beneath it, conceding to its terms as we conceded to anaesthetic for our various childhood maladies – tonsils, ears, teeth. Learned not to notice – not consciously – the fierceness of her compensations: the pull and push of need, the nearness and distance of love. We learned, as children do, to behave in ways that might make her, if not happy, then less unhappy. We were still doing this when she died, too young, twelve years ago, and in some ways we haven't stopped.

In the years before we'd learned some of the facts – the earlier marriage, the cruel husband, the stolen baby – but the flesh and bones of her life were buried with her in autumn-damp soil. What she left was a fine, opaque pattern like the ones she pinned over fabric to make our clothes, a movable outline that refused to be fixed. We began to ask questions then, wanting the answers she'd never have given. But our knowledge was partial so our questions were too; with every answer the lines shifted, and with them the shape of her.

This is what we didn't understand, not then: that the past had gripped and confounded her, stalked her dreams. That every day of her life after her son was taken, she would sift through the memory of it, every terrible second. Turning each in her hand, looking for ways she might have changed them. But always she would be stuck at the image of the man, her husband, the terrible smile as he entered the train carriage, walked towards her, pulled Peter from her arms. When she dreamed of her lost son she would dream of his father. He would always be walking towards her, wearing that smile.

In my head, it happens like this: she is standing behind the high glass counter of The Palms Café in Queen Street. It is lunchtime and busy, but she is momentarily still, flicking at a drift of flour on her apron – or perhaps she is tucking back a lick of wayward hair and checking her lipstick – quickly, covertly – in the mirrored panel behind her. At sixteen she has the celebrated curves of a movie star, 36-24-36, and is told she is just as beautiful. Of course, she doesn't believe it – though she'd like to. She doesn't want people to think she is vain. Her father, especially. He'd be disappointed, she knows, at any sign of vanity, any sign of conceit.

As she leans into the mirror she touches a forefinger to her lips – they are full, crimson-tinted – and sees suddenly she is being watched. It is the same man, the same eyes she had felt on her earlier that week as she carried trays with cups and teapots and scones between tables. He is darkly good-looking, and well dressed – pressed trousers, a starched white shirt. He is not a boy. A smile lurks at the corners of his mouth and it is the smile of a worldly man. A smile of intent. Her stomach flips like a fish on a hook.

Her hands move once more to her apron, she smooths imaginary creases, then turns to the serving bay. She has to remind herself to breathe. But there is safety in the plates of piled food; she risks a glance from lowered eyes. This is what she sees: his dark beauty. That it has made him dangerous. His eyes. Charisma and the possibility not just of vanity but of toughness. Of passion. She sees all this now, but seeing is not knowing. Otherwise, why would she risk that glance, a faint movement of her eyes and lips, a telltale dip of long lashes? She slides plates onto a nearby table and as she spins away he appraises her legs, her fine ankles.

This is what she doesn't know: she is an ingénue, an innocent. From this perspective, sixty years on, and even then. Even then, though she has lived through depression and the effects of a war that didn't quite come to her. It has been her luck to be born and to live in this half-forgotten town in a country on the edge of the world's consciousness. Everything is far from here – the shattered cities of Europe, her father's beloved English fields, the queues of the hungry and the homeless. Until now. The world of adults, of ravaged cultures and displacement, of sex and power, has just walked into her life in the shape of Minas Panayotis Preneas. Michael, or Mick, to his friends. He has come from the war-weary Greek island of Kythera to make his fortune and his life. At thirty-four he is literally twice her age, experienced, hardened, hungry. She is a naively beautiful girl from the poor and unformed outer suburbs of Brisbane. She doesn't stand a chance.

There are pockets of modern Brisbane that still retain a sense of the older town, the subtropical British outpost it was in the beginning and the 'big country town' it was when my mother grew up here. That phrase – *big country town* – was how her generation described it, and until about ten years ago there was still enough of that quality for me to understand why. Weather, geography, history, circumstance: they all contribute to a certain attitude – Brisbane's was a bit brash, a bit slow, a bit defensive. Hothouse too: everyone had links to everyone else through school, work, family. Up until ten years ago, we could joke that reading the social pages of *The Courier-Mail* was like going through the family album.

My mother's Brisbane, in my mind, is the Brisbane of her youth – roughly, I suppose, between 1944 and 1960 – and though she grew up on its dusty outskirts, I can see it and feel it most in its inner-city streets. No matter that the town has been cavalier with the wrecking ball and careless of the fragility of tongue-and-groove and iron lacework. If a street boasts even a semblance of aged sandstone or an arched façade or a verandah more than fifty years old, then it retains for me the air my mother breathed.

It's there around the Treasury building and the Lands building facing each other across the park and its soaring statue of Queen Victoria; it's in the arcades – Rowes and Brisbane, with their marble and mosaic tiling and wood-panelled shopfronts; it swirls around the Story Bridge and the old streets of New Farm, where jacaranda and hibiscus and palm fronds still stray across iron lacework verandahs. It has a sound, that air: a tram and its metallic lurch, a bell on a pulled cord, paperboys on corners. And a smell: buttery slabs of soap, malt in a milkshake, hops boiling in the brewery at the northern end of the bridge.

I follow her figure through all these places now; a brush of full skirt past the bank at the top of Queen Street; a tap of high heels near the shops in the Valley where the tram stops. A flash of dark eyes, the turn of wrist or ankle as she boards a bus, lifts a cup, steps into the dim cave of a cinema. Tantalising glimpses of the woman she was before she was my mother; the shape of the life she had planned before Michael appeared with his version of it.

These flashes of her from a shadowy Brisbane have always been the easy ones to construct. It is early in 1947; I know how the town was shaped, the line of it, the way girls and women dressed. My mother looks like so many other girls hurrying to work or pausing at Bayard's window, checking the line of her stockings or hem. She might have stepped from the tram fully formed, without background or history or family. Her olive skin and her eyes, her shapely limbs, her bearing, utterly her own and not inherited from others. She is just her singular self.

But of course there is a father and a mother in the life she has outside these streets, and a home loud with siblings and money stretched too tight. She is the eldest and already there are five more – soon there will be six – in this thin-skinned wooden house at Cannon Hill. It crouches among other wooden homes near cow paddocks recently occupied by the US Army; she and her closest sister, Evelyn, have been warned by their father to stay away from the camp, from the servicemen with their easy smiles. Now that the soldiers have gone, the sisters miss the frisson of danger – even though, fearing their father's wrath, they'd rarely ventured close.

My mother's younger self lives here, or that is how it seems: after work she steps through the door and becomes a girl compliant and almost undifferentiated from her siblings and their scramble for space and air and enough to eat. She is part of them. Perhaps this is why I can't see her here, in the clamour and crush of her family. She blends with them immediately, helping her mother in the kitchen, seeing to the other children. The younger ones adore her. She shares the chores of bathing and feeding and entertaining them; from her they get the gentle attention they crave from their mother, and they cherish her. As adults they will talk about it endlessly: how she mothered them. Their voices yielding, soft.

But despite all this I can't see her childhood face, or the shape of her among them, I can't see the clothes she changes into after work or what she does with her hair. It is true there is not one photograph of her as a child in this house or the others the family lived in – no baby or school photo, no carefully arranged family picture, no informal snap. Nothing. In this family there was no money for such things, they would have been an extravagance, unthinkable.

Still, some families found pennies for photographs. I think of my father's Swedish childhood, provincial and far from rich – he too wore cast-off clothing and ate what was grown in the yard – but it is all recorded in black and white and carefully preserved. There they are in the album: random images of boys at play, posed pictures of his mother with her sons. I can look at these photographs and animate them, see the burst of action or laughter that follows – my father breaking free of his mother's arm or chasing the dog across the cobbled yard or elbowing his brother off the front step where they've been made to stand and smile.

Not so my mother. I can't animate her here in her home, so for me, she *does* spring fully formed from that tram in the city, as though she was born sixteen. From the outset I've known certain things about her childhood – the poverty, the truncated education, her love of books and learning – but this knowledge alone gave me no hint of her spirit, of the child she had been. Was it because of the absence of photographic evidence? Or because she was born in 1930, a decade in which childhood might have been arbitrary, especially among the poor?

Just twelve years after the Armistice, Australia was a place uneasy and staggering between two world wars: loss was still thick in the air, and the absence of young men in houses and streets still a shock, to the eye and the heart. So perhaps there was no inclination, when she was a small child, to commemorate anything other than terrible loss, and survival that was nearly as terrible. I don't know. I sit at my desk and I'm surrounded by images of family and friends that remind me I am tied not just to others but to other times, that remind me of who I am. So to me, the lack of childhood pictures of my mother suggests an equation: no pictures = no childhood. In a life that would come to be defined by absence, this is an absence too.

There is only one photograph of my mother that she let my father hang in the house. Apart from their wedding portrait, which stood on the duchess in their bedroom; or the occasional snap someone would frame from a birthday or a picnic, Mum with her sisters or holding a grandchild, that she'd frown and prop on the sideboard for a few weeks before tucking it away. She hated being photographed, hated the results. *I look terrible in that,* she'd say, dismissing the latest print with barely a look and walking off towards the kitchen. Now I can see the camera might have perpetuated the suffering, the residue of pain she could scrub from her real face every morning, disguise with Oil of Ulan every night. As for us, we saw in those pictures only what we wanted to see then, projecting our own need for her happiness into the frame.

The one photograph was different. It was taken, we were told, for her twenty-first birthday – two years after Peter disappeared, a year after Sharon was born – in one of the studios you could find in every city in the fifties and sixties, their windows testament to the power of colour tinting, of vanity, of the desire to construct and edit our memories and our lives. To our need to commemorate youth or happiness or beauty. The one photograph of our mother encapsulates all of this; it would be no surprise if, as she told us, the photographer had displayed it for weeks in his own window in Queen Street.

A casual observer might be drawn in simply by her face. Soft brown eyes beneath dark brows and hair, red rosebud lips that promise nothing or something, depending on your angle. She is wearing a white gypsy blouse embroidered with tiny red roses around a smocked neckline, and pearl drop earrings. She might be sixteen and she might be twenty-six.

But for me the photo's real impact is in its composition. She is not facing the camera squarely; her body is turned sideways and she's looking over her shoulder at us, her head tilted a little. Another subject might have made the pose coquettish, or played the imp or the siren. But this young woman turns that notion upside-down, because, of course, she's not looking forward to something but back, her eyes filled with longing rather than anticipation. No one could argue about her beauty in this photograph – that's probably why she liked it – but to me it speaks of sorrow, of all she'd endured in her life and all that is at stake. She is at once the girl Michael wanted, the woman my father loved, the grieving, wistful mother we adored. Still vulnerable, still innocent despite everything, a woman of infinite tenderness and quiet fury.

We all have copies of this photograph; Dad had them framed for us. For the past year I've kept mine on this old table, and it's become the focus of all the questions I have and all the answers I don't. I've taken to talking to it, to her. I whisper: *all the things you didn't say, all the things we didn't know.* I look into the eyes that hide her secrets and hold them. They glint like glass, like water. Is it the photographer's artificial shine, like the deft blush of pink on cheeks and the moist rubied lips? Or were her eyes brim full that day of everything she'd buried, all the pain dammed up behind them, the shame we confused with indifference all our lives?

Michael is back at The Palms two days later, then again the following week. In a town clothed by ration cards, he must have been hard to miss. His shirts and trousers are clean and pressed, as if he's just plucked them from the diminished rack at Barry and Roberts, further up Queen Street. She sees that he drinks coffee, thick and black, like the other men he meets here. They all drink and talk.

This day, a Monday, she looks up from cleaning the milkshake machine to find him staring at her from a booth towards the front of the café. She averts her eyes, works the cloth fiercely around the base of the machine. His smile: there is mischief in it, he might be just a flirty boy. When he smiles at her again as she passes two days later – his third visit in three days – it seems churlish or even rude not to smile back. He's a customer, after all. A regular.

He already knows her name, the one she's given herself. She is not Mimi here but Yvonne. He says it one day – Y-*vonne* – the weight on the *vonne*, and something wakes inside her. It is as if she is being called, her real self summoned. Not *EE*-vonne, the

Y hardened in the Australian way. In Michael's pronunciation, in the play of syllables, he has brought a new woman into being. Different. This happens in an instant, but she knows immediately she is changed. She doesn't know who Yvonne is yet but she knows who she isn't: a creature trapped beneath the humid hand of this town. Beneath turgid domestic jobs, waitressing, penury. The life her mother lives, beige-toned, the days grinding away to sameness. So when Michael offers Yvonne a lift home on his motorbike one afternoon in spring, she accepts, and with her hands on his waist – small for a man – and watching houses, trees, trams roar past, she can see the possibilities.

Her mother and her father, then. An odd union she has never understood: they are chalk and cheese, night and day. She loves them but is slightly repelled by them, certain her life will be different from theirs.

Veronica, after whom she is named, is called Ronnie and it suits her: she is tough and irascible, her harsh vowels as tireless as her hands in the wash tub or the kitchen. Her forebears are solidly working class – shopkeepers, hoteliers, carpenters, coal-lumpers, and she has inherited their clamorous voices, their lusty laughs. Everything about Veronica is loud. My mother – she is called Mimi, or Minnie, to differentiate her – shrinks from her shrillness in shops or in the street, hoping no one she knows is in earshot. She is terrified it may be genetic.

But Mimi's view of her father is very different. He is, she decides early, a gentleman, with a respect for knowledge, for the proper and the good. He loves to read and to paint, he loves music, and with these he tries to make up for early poverty, a curtailed education, the potential that has been lost. This, she decides, is what has survived in her father: honesty and honour. She sees the efforts he makes to uphold them. Her father, she decides, has been well named.

She understands too that her father's life and outlook had been shaped not just by disappointment but by pain – a boyhood accident on a bad-tempered horse. A steel brace now strapped and gripped his spine: a stiff and unyielding contraption, controlling and grim. And this is how he might appear to others – it's how he appeared to me as a child – but Mimi has a different understanding of her father and his disappointments. He is not stiff, but upright. Not controlling, but strong. If he is often dour and unsmiling, if he frowns over the watercolours he paints in all the greens of England, or over the vegetables he tends or the opera he turns his ear to on the wireless, and if his demeanour sometimes crumples and he shouts and smacks them, she reminds herself of his heroism: in enduring his pain, in missing England, in facing the incorrigible Ronnie over the porridge pot at breakfast every morning.

Like my mother, I was often embarrassed by Ronnie as well, this too-loud, too-plain, too-coarse grandmother who bore no resemblance to the benevolent, grey-haired versions in school readers or *The Famous Five*. They were wise and loving creatures who plied their grandchildren with fruit cake and kisses and let them rummage in dusty boxes in the attic. Pulled them onto their generous laps and told them marvellous stories, pressed a pound into their palms as they went reluctantly home. Ronnie was never that kind of grandmother. So it was easy to accept my mother's take on her, almost all my life: Ronnie was selfish, she was rough, she was too much. And poor Ernest, on the other hand – all that pain and Ronnie into the bargain.

But in truth I didn't notice my grandparents much at all. And neither did I know the origins of the resentments that coloured the relationship between them and my mother. An undercurrent of anger ran beneath the determined and regular attention she paid them, the sedulous devotion as they grew old and more withdrawn and sullen. Every week in their later years, my mother and her sisters cooked, cleaned and shopped for them; tried to coax Veronica into a bath or to change her clothes, to persuade Ernest to open a window in the stifling summer kitchen. To take a gentle turn around the garden, to page through the books or magazines they'd brought, to try the casserole. They would be rewarded, at times, with a quick lash from Veronica's sharp fingernails at their arms or hands; more often with blank refusals from both. At home later my mother would mutter darkly: her parents' dourness, their stubborn descent into gloom, their eternal complaints. And mostly: Veronica's heartlessness, her lack of interest and gratitude and grace.

I watched and listened and absorbed this odd mix of filial love and duty and anger. Somewhere I must have registered the edge in my mother's emotions that her sisters didn't have. Like her they were mystified and frustrated by their parents, their seeming complicity with the ravages of age, their deep suspicion of happiness. But my mother was both more wounded and more embittered by these encounters. *They won't help themselves*, she'd say in the car on the way home, pursing her lips and turning her face to the window. And over cappuccino with her sisters: *They won't go out, they won't have any noise, they shut themselves off.* The girls would nod and butter their scones. Then: *Not like Old Gran*, Evelyn would say with a grin. *Remember how she loved the girls dancing the cancan in your kitchen, Mimi? They'd flip up their skirts and she'd pretend to be outraged. Then she'd say, do it again!*

They'd all laugh and nod and someone would ask for the jam. Then my mother would grimace. *The girls wouldn't be dancing*, she'd say, *if Mum was in the house.*

Every few months over recent years, I've driven down from the city to talk to two of my mother's sisters, Evelyn and Ann, in the bayside suburb where they both still live. We'd sit in Evelyn's kitchen and, over egg and lettuce sandwiches and strong tea, I've asked some of the questions I had wanted to ask my mother. I suppose I was prepared for reluctance, for wavering, and phrased my questions carefully, unsure at first of what was trespass and what was not. Unsure if they too had locked their memories and opinions into an unbreachable vault, for their sister's sake or for their own. So I was surprised by their willingness, not just to remember but to consider and analyse, and to return to the same conversations again and again as I tried to come to grips with what I heard.

Their thoughts emerged slowly, as they might from people long inured to keeping secrets, people convinced it was the right thing to do. It wasn't that they hesitated, or didn't want to speak; more that the information, so long buried, took a while to process and to surface. They'd speak quietly, in a kind of hush, as if the words themselves could still be hurtful, or loaded, or as if their sister might still hear them, years after her death. In that atmosphere I received each sentence as a gift, gratefully, struck not just by their candour but by the fact I was hearing the stories at all.

In the end their knowledge of my mother's first marriage was limited, fragmented by their youth at the time and their sister's determined silence. But it was their version of my mother's youth and childhood that unsettled me. At first I tried to ignore the growing disparities between their stories and those my mother told, the impressions I'd absorbed of my grandparents' role in her early life. It took me a long time to concede my mother's stories were not immovable truths; it felt disloyal, treacherous even, to question her version, to disassemble my own acceptance of it. To do so meant admitting not just the fallibility of that version but my complicity in believing it, my need to believe it. Gradually, after a lifetime of dealing in certainties – the plain facts of journalism, my own black and white views – I began to feel the nausea of *un*certainty. Not just about my mother's version of her childhood but my version of my own, and with it my sense of myself. It was the first of many concessions I had to make, truths I had to acknowledge, before this story revealed itself, gave itself up, settled into its shape.

Michael is her secret, at first. They confine themselves to flirtations at the café, the occasional ride home. She will not let him take her to the door, but slips from the bike near the train station, waving him away. She knows instinctively her father will disapprove, of the motorbike and the man – his age, his foreignness. He will disapprove of Michael's charm, will not trust it. She's his eldest daughter, sensible, dutiful. He would prefer she brought home a local lad, someone who speaks the King's English. Someone her own age, rather than his. She knows all this.

But her relationship with Michael makes her bold. The attention of a mature man changes the way she sees herself: she is a woman, not a girl, with a new awareness of her powers. With each meeting her confidence grows. She has never been self-assured but she listens to him tell her how beautiful she is, her eyes, her lips, and it's hard not to believe it; his own eyes traverse her body slowly from her ankles to her brows and there is no doubt what he is thinking. She shivers, feeling her skin tighten beneath her clothes, a stirring she has never felt before. It makes her reckless. She decides to take him home to meet her parents, her siblings, her grandmother. A risky enough venture for the woman Yvonne, but more so for the girl Mimi, who lives in that home and who, among her family, has no other name.

It is as she had thought it would be: her father, braced by the steel in his back and his serial disappointments, is all formality. He shakes Michael's hand. She notices his clean shirt and carefully parted hair, wonders what the effort has cost him. And feels stung, momentarily, by her love of him, her dour, decent father.

Veronica slips up beside her husband like a girl. She is struck by Michael's beauty, Yvonne can see that. She smiles as she accepts his offering, a fish rather than flowers, a fish freshly caught. This will become a pattern, this gift of a fish; it impresses Veronica because, as she says, you can't eat flowers. But on this first day she grips the parcel, winks at her daughter and offers tea.

Evelyn eyes Michael shyly from a doorway. Mimi can read her thoughts: he is so different from her own beau, Edward, a boy from Kangaroo Point who dreams of horses, of the vast plains of the west. He is a straight talker, Edward, and says what he means, and he watches over Evelyn, over them both, especially at the Morningside picture theatre where boys swagger and cuss. She knows immediately he won't like Michael.

And from her corner her grandmother, Eliza, frowns at them all, at the wide-eyed younger children sidling into the room, at Michael. He is too pretty for her liking, too sure, Mimi can tell. *Beware Greeks bearing gifts*, Eliza tells her later, nodding like a sage. But it's already too late: she's in love. Besotted. And she doesn't even care that Eliza won't approve, that no one will. The only approval she needs is Michael's.

Over the following months Evelyn watches Michael, and sees he has begun a campaign. It is a word she has heard a lot in her wartime childhood and it enters her head whenever he appears at their door with his gifts and his grin. This campaign has its own weapons – flirtation and charm, and he includes the whole family in their wide sweep. He uses compliments and winks, fresh fish and Greek sweets, offers of rides on his motorbike. For the twins, not yet at school, his visits are treats, thrilling. They love the bike, its throaty roar, the precarious air that rushes into their faces when he takes them up the street.

Ernie and Geoffrey, newly adolescent, find Michael irresistible, his mix of sophisticated big brother and playful father. But the things that impress the younger ones – his swagger, the exotic sounds that spill from his lips – are the things Evelyn finds unsettling. Later in her life she will remember thinking: he's too *smooth*. Like her siblings she is shy and uncertain about the world, and though she likes him – she can't help it – his cockiness unnerves her. So she stands back, watches him as she might watch a beautiful old lion that has found its way into the house, with a mixture of awe and anxiety and distrust.

All the same she keeps her own counsel about him and isn't rude – laughs politely at his insistent offers to find her a *good Greek boyfriend* – because she can see her sister is smitten. In Michael's company Mimi is a different creature; everything – her skin, the way she speaks – seems plumped out with love. Some light has been flicked on behind her eyes; they follow Michael's every move and at the time Evelyn can only think of the word 'covetous'. That's it: as if her sister wants to possess every part of him, jealous of the things he touches and looks at, the glass in his hand, the moon. He makes the local boys, even the ones with jobs and money for the movies, look like lambs.

Mimi's seventeenth birthday at the end of October draws some kind of line in her life. Something is liberated in her; some shell or armour is cast off. She is no longer tentative about Michael, doesn't try to hide her infatuation. She talks endlessly to Evelyn about his plans to run cafés, to make money and buy a house, maybe flats; compares his looks to heart-throb actors and singers – Harry Belafonte, Anthony Quinn, Caruso. She loves these dark, exotic men, she's told Evelyn a hundred times.

She gives no hint of apology about Michael's age or background or the increasingly frequent dates and visits. There is a steeliness that has always slept in Mimi's veins; she calls on it when she and Evelyn endure unfair punishments or their parents' harsh words or when there is no money for her little brothers to join the cricket team. She will say to her mother: *that's not fair.* As younger children they'd been quiet, would never have answered back, but now she lets this steel, this determination, emerge. It allows her to step through the cloud of unease about Michael that has been gradually thickening throughout the house. *He's a silver tongue, that Mick*, Ronnie says. *A palaverer.* But Mimi doesn't want to hear. Her mind is set. She grins at Evelyn's shock when, one night, Ronnie and Ernest raise an objection to her late nights and she tells them promptly to *mind your own business.*

Mind your own business. Evelyn laughed softly when she told me this, watching my hand snap to my mouth as hers had done that long ago night. *She was a bit rebellious, your mum*, she said. *Never rude. But determined.* I'd seen the determination, all right – in an argument she would never let go – but I'd always seen it as a facet of her stoicism, the quiet strength she used through years of hard work and childrearing and illness. But *rebellious* was the last word I'd have used about her. For as long as I could remember she'd been scornful of the notion, and wary of any signs of it in me. *I wish I'd known that*, I said to Evelyn, *when I was sixteen.*

But at sixteen I knew nothing of my mother's history. Not consciously – though in our bodies we'd all felt the shadow of her injury and were marked by it at birth. And though I know that now, I would have furiously denied it when I was young, intent on living out the version I thought was my own. That's what you do, as a child: you take whatever is at hand and mould it into something bright or safe or consoling.

So it isn't until someone says to you, when you are an adult, that there must have been a darkness in your childhood, there must have been a sense of absence, always, that you begin to think of this and the melancholy that, in some way, you must have felt too.

Did I? I am tempted to say that, looking back, there was some child-shaped grief that lived in all the rooms of the house. We couldn't have said that then. If it was there, if she carried it around disguised as something else, it wasn't immediately noticeable to a small child. To any of us. If she bent sad eyes towards us in the mornings as we hurried through breakfast and our turns at the washing up, we didn't see them. We tore past her, out through the laundry and into the yard, where we lived largely in or beneath the trees – mango and mulberry, fig and banana, loquat and macadamia. Or in the abandoned chook pen, or the shell of an ancient and roofless car. The steps to the old flats, the dank area beneath the workshop, the open grass among all of this – house, flats, trees, workshop, garage – was a world made new every day, full of possibility. Any weight of sadness was ground into the dirt beneath the trees, or hidden behind high branches and a screen of leaves, or cried out in tears when we fell. But we rarely fell.

It would be years until I realised it: the sense of melancholy around my mother was one of suffering. As a young woman I understood that women suffered and mothers in particular; they suffered and there was nothing you could do to avoid it. It was something to do with their place among children and men, some punishment for whatever unspecified wrong they had done. It would be years after I became a mother myself before I began to understand the sin my mother was punishing herself for.

She lies awake in her bed. The bright beam from an occasional car or motorbike traces an arc across the ceiling, and her eyes follow as if the line of light is a signpost to elsewhere. Then they return to the dark centre of the room.

Beside her Evelyn sleeps like a child, her face innocent and unmarked by the kind of thoughts she herself is having. She half pities, half envies that innocence. But she can't help what she's feeling. It is as if Michael has breathed into her and brought her to life. Her newly awakened eyes see differently, all her senses are open to the air, they sting and tremble with it. She feels his nearness as well as his absence like this, as physical sensations, a ripple of pleasure or emptiness through her whole body.

He wants to take her away with him. Far away, to north Queensland, where men like him, he says, can get rich off sugar or by feeding the mad hungry cane cutters, their sugar-mad wives. The north, he'd said to her that day, toying with her hair, is juicy with money. She'd smiled at the words he plucked from his limited English, but then he got serious. *You should come and see,* agapi mou, he said, *for a holiday, you know. A week, maybe two.* He paused, winked. *Don't worry, I'll take care of you.*

She'd looked at him, exhilarated at the impossibility of it. They were leaning together in a café booth, so close she could smell his skin, crushed almonds and tobacco and yes, sugar. In that moment she knew she would go.

Now she turns in her bed and closes her eyes against the inevitable thought of her father. The way this news would break across his face, setting to stone the unsmiling mouth and eyes. The terrible disapproval. But it has always been like this: dejection has fossilised in him, so that each new bafflement or misfortune registers only as a familiar ache, perhaps in his back, or in his throat. When they come his words will be sharp flints that strike against her own, and they will hurt. But she has learned from him and his flinty heart, the way it has closed over hard decisions, over all the deprivations of their childhood, and she knows she can make her own heart do the same. Just briefly. Just as long as it takes her to leave.

She suspects her baby is conceived in the sleeper compartment Michael had booked for the train journey north. In May, when she is back from her tropical holiday in seaside Cardwell, the pregnancy is confirmed. I imagine her amid the chloroform and old leather smells of a doctor's surgery in town, her lovely face pale though she has known this news, known it in her cells, for weeks. She sits there wordlessly in the room with its stoppered bottles and trays and air of trepidation, watches the shape the doctor's lips make as he speaks, the puckered O of *positive*. When she gets outside that's all she can see, his face and his stony eyes, smug with the knowledge they have, all his assumptions about her.

Well, she thinks, and a small smile creeps to her lips. Well, all his assumptions are wrong. She puts a hand to her belly, to the place where their child is growing, and feels a flush of euphoria and pride. Their child, Michael's and hers. This is her first reaction, this sense of pleasure. She can be smug too.

She walks slowly up Queen Street, glancing down as she does: breasts, belly, legs. Outwardly there is little sign that her world has changed. Her belly seems flat – there is no tell-tale roundness yet, though nausea swirls there every morning – but she feels her breasts bulge uncomfortably against her blouse. No one, not even her parents, has noticed a thing.

Her parents. As she moves up the street she imagines their faces, the scene when she tells them. She'll get around her mother, she thinks. But her father. She can see his bitter surprise, the way shock, or wrath, twists his mouth. His anger doesn't scare her any more, she's grown out of that, but there is the matter of respect. And honour. Those words. From beneath the excitement she feels a swell of agitation that might be morning sickness or might be fear she will lose his esteem completely.

The kitchen suddenly hushes, and the young ones are sent outside.

Evelyn remembers the to-do: *She should never have been allowed to go away*, her grandmother says. Ronnie volleys: *Why didn't* you *stop her?* And Ernest turns his disappointed gaze from his daughter to his wife. *No, it's true, she shouldn't have gone.* Slaps his palm on the table. *She's bloody well half his age, Ron.*

Mimi tries for calm. Tells them she's going back to the north, back to Michael. He has a snack bar now in Cairns, with a flat above it. She'll work in the shop, they'll make good money, better than here. And he'll marry her, he's as good as said. She tries to sound confident, mature. Avoids her father's eyes, except when she reminds him Veronica was the same age when *they* married. Seventeen.

The gauntlet is thrown; he doesn't pick it up. It's a kind of victory, but right then and in the following days she can't locate any of that early euphoria, the excitement of this new and bodily link to Michael, of the sudden end to the life she'd been pining to leave. If there's doubt beneath her confidence she doesn't mention it to anyone.

She slips into the knot of fate so easily, so fast. Ten months: the time she's known him. But she's greedy now for a real life, ready. She buys a ticket for *The Sunlander*, and counts down the days.

The far north of the state – and of Australia – is frontier land in 1948. Wild, largely unbroken, the rainforest shuffling its feet at everyone's door, at every clearing, threatening chaos if human diligence should lapse. Cyclones, floods, crocodiles, heat. And opportunity, now that it's safe from the danger of enemy invasion that drove many away in the war, now that the wharves are busy and the mines have been cleared and victory has brought everyone back to the streets.

She steps from the train into a wall of humidity. It's like a woollen blanket. She's allergic to wool, can't bear it on her skin. Sweat springs from her as though she's been punctured; she feels the dampness in her armpits and on her scalp and looks around, dismayed, embarrassed. But Michael has a forearm to his own glistening face and is urging her towards the gate. She moves slowly, as if she's pushing through water.

The town itself is at once foreign and familiar. At first she feels wary, shy. The streets are not unlike home: dirt roads, simple wooden buildings crouching beside them. Houses on stilts, flimsy, their timbers at the mercy of hard sun and harder rain. But that is all at eye level. If she lifts her face and breathes she will sense immediately how utterly different this place is, how strange. How its foliage and its animals and even its people might grow wild here, because there is nothing to stop them. There is no restraint; nothing is pulled back, nothing is hesitant. All around the town mountains and rainforest lean in, they loom over rooflines and dominate the sky. And beneath them, beyond the straggling houses, the green and endless stretch of sugar cane.

They walk in beating sunshine, carrying their cases. It is only a couple of streets away, Michael assures her, but it feels much further. She glances at the people who swing past her, tries to gauge their faces. Looks for some hint of the lives being lived here, a suggestion of kindness or toughness or just a readiness to nod to a stranger. But the town itself competes for her attention: the fig trees in the street, the dusty shopfronts, a dank, water-logged smell that reminds her of old sweat. Finally Michael stops at a door in a row of shopfronts in Grafton Street – a drapery, a bank, then a snack bar. Above their wide awnings are the balustraded balconies of tiny flats and offices.

Michael is beaming at her. She is, she realises, home.

Her new life begins immediately. There is no preamble, no settling in. She is put to work in the shop, cooking, serving, cleaning up, and it is hard and physical and the hours long. The work itself doesn't daunt her – she has worked in cafés on and off since she left childhood – but something in Michael does. Overnight, her sweet-talking paramour has turned into her boss. It takes her by surprise: the edge to his voice when he speaks to her around customers, an impatience when he asks for eggs or tomatoes or if she is too slow adding up the bill. She tries to learn quickly, how thinly to cut the potatoes, how many chips in a serve. But the shop is busy and the pregnancy slows her down. In north Queensland the heat starts to build in early spring, just as her belly begins to balloon, so the heaviness she feels is doubled.

She tries not to notice his off-handedness. Works quietly beside him as he plunges baskets of fish into boiling oil, flips hamburgers and eggs, drags crates of soft drink and milk to the low fridge where she bends to arrange them. Men from the local Greek community come and go; if it's quiet he will stop and drink coffee with them, the black syrupy liquid that looks like tar. She watches from behind the counter, trying to interpret their gabble, as her mother would call it. Tries not to feel excluded. In the sound of their voices and their laughter, the relaxed arrangement of their limbs, she sees what she is missing, the easy affection.

And there's this: the looks the men give her, the unashamed appraisals as she brings the coffee Michael calls for. Her cheeks burn as she walks away. She imagines them thinking: *easy Australian girl*. She'd assumed they'd be married by now, but Michael makes excuses: the shop is too busy, can't she see he is trying to make money? But by September she can no longer tolerate it. She thinks of her family, their opinions and expectations, but also of the girls she grew up with, her sisters and cousins – the white dresses and veils they'd planned, the bridesmaids, the flowers. And insists on a wedding, just a quiet ceremony, but in a church. Not the Godless government office Michael suggests. She wants this union to be blessed, even if she doesn't know the pastor or the words he will speak over their heads. The marriage will feel real, a solid thing, if it's solemnised in a church, even if there are no bridesmaids, no dress, no party.

They are married on a Friday morning, in a Methodist church as her parents had been, a squat building of reassuring brick. It isn't the wedding her sisters will have, the one she'd imagined in quiet moments at The Palms, when everything seemed possible. They repeat simple vows and sign the marriage register. There is no shower of rice as they emerge through the arched doorway into the glare of an ordinary, unchanged Friday, no excited kisses or handshakes, no camera flash. But that doesn't stop the rush of happiness she feels at the cheap gold band on her finger, at her new legal status and name. Mrs Yvonne Preneas. At last.

This sustains her for a while, but in the months ahead she will remember these moments in the church, his accented vows, their names signed together, and she will be stunned that he hid himself so well. That she could know a man, marry him, carry his child, with no notion that he could not read or write. The knowledge is not sudden, but accumulates in her: he can manage a signature, simple arithmetic, and there are words he knows by heart, but she begins to notice the letters that go unanswered until a younger Greek friend is around, the labels he asks him to read, a notice from the landlord he thrusts into her hands as if he isn't interested. She feels the shock of this knowledge in her body, but especially in the part of her that is still hungry for learning, still mourns the loss of it, the part that is proud, nevertheless, of what her brain can do. She feels a new flush of sadness for him, and embarrassment, and disquiet.

The only real change the marriage makes is inside her head. It's just one word and it's almost enough: *respectable*. As if the marriage has made her legitimate, as well as her baby. But it hasn't brought the old Michael back to her; if anything, he is colder and more distant than before. Several nights a week after the café closes, he goes to the card tables down near the wharf. She has no idea what time he comes in; exhaustion sinks her in sleep so deep she hears and feels nothing. In the morning she tries to ignore the sour twist to his mouth when he wakes.

As her eighteenth birthday comes and goes at the end of October with no acknowledgement from him, she begins to wonder if the fault is with her. The bulbous shape this baby has made of her, the puffiness in her face, the shapeless dresses. He doesn't even look at her the way he once did; his hand rarely brushes her face or her thigh. When something goes wrong – they run out of lettuce, she isn't quick enough wrapping the fish or clearing the plates – and he swears at her in Greek, she blames herself or the heat or the long hours at the stove.

In the last month of her pregnancy his absences begin to lengthen. He closes the shop early and disappears with some of the Greek men to Innisfail, not returning until morning. Saturday night turns into Sunday and still he is not home. Sometimes he is happy as a lark when he returns to the tiny flat above the shop, he is all tender embraces and smiles and caresses, gentle. These times feel like a reward. But more often his face is shadowed, his eyes hard and looking for any failure in her, any lack. She tries to accommodate this mood; makes sure her hair is combed, her cheap maternity smocks clean and the flat presentable. Tries to ignore the hard line of his mouth, his dismissiveness. But she quickly learns it isn't enough, that perfection is not what he wants then, that in fact he needs *imperfection* in her, something to rail against, to punish. Still, she tries; her fear and youth dictate it. But it makes no difference. She endures the shouting and insults, the frightening anger. When the inevitable happens and the shouts turn into slaps she is almost, almost expecting it.

My mother was so young and knew so little. About Michael, about the world of men. She didn't know that she'd stumbled into a marriage whose patterns had already been set, by Michael himself and the patriarchal island culture he came from. Even sixty years later, when I walked around Kythera with my sister, I could see our mother's youth and energy and innocence would have been no match for the combined forces of Michael and his history, could have no impact on them. Partly, he was a product of his ancient culture and birthplace, and the traditions that gripped and clung to it, like the vines that clutched at the walls and roof of his family house. It was, like many others on that old, barren island, the house of a peasant, of a family and a population hopelessly entwined with the poverty of their land and circumstances.

As Greece writhed in economic meltdown in 2011, it didn't look like much had changed among the shattered houses of Michael's village and the stores with their half-empty shelves. Men and boys at the *kafeneon* were still making plans to leave, just as, in the decades before and after Michael left the island, war and deprivation propelled the young men away. They took their culture with them, to Australia and England and America – some a love of dancing, or of talk and backgammon and cards and strong coffee. Michael brought all these, but in him they were exaggerated: his dancing was expert, his gambling serious and compulsive. My mother hadn't seen that in their courtship, nor his propensity to cruelty, his casual arrogance towards women.

She knew nothing of his culture, not at first. She didn't know he came from a place and a time in which some men might subjugate their wives, might see it as their right to hit them, to see them as chattels, as servants and providers of sons. She didn't know that, among the men of the Greek diaspora, especially the young and the lonely, gambling had often gone beyond the social cards and backgammon of the *kafeneon* to the dangerous illegal dens, where fortunes and lives were wagered. She didn't know the humiliation of illiteracy, that the inability to read, in any language, could make a man sly.

Michael was a bad-tempered and committed gambler long before he met my mother. There'd been at least one fracas with a knife at an Ipswich gambling house. And through the extra-ordinary grapevine of the immigrant Greek community – the café owners and fruit growers and cane cutters – Michael knew the gambling tables of the north were busy and lucrative, a powerful lure to the tropics, a whole new landscape of luck.

So even a grown-up woman might not have noticed the clash of time and culture she'd walked into: a man like Michael in a place like Queensland after the war. Despite victory it was conservative and austere, and a new moral Puritanism was in the air, one that punished women for any perceived sexual transgression, that insisted on the chaste wife and mother but ignored the violence inflicted on them behind closed doors.

But love and naivety had blinded her: she was strong, she had decided, she could make it work. Besides, it was official, she was Yvonne Preneas. A name to make a dream, to build a life.

The marriage certificate reveals how determined she was in her naivety, how thoroughly she had become this new person. This Yvonne. In shedding her old name she had shed her old skin, her old self, assuming instead the name of a woman with prospects, an exotic one like Yvonne de Carlo, or Gina Lollobrigida, whose posters were splashed outside cinemas then, whose faces hers had been likened to. Dark-haired actresses who played roles too. Who lived different lives.

Their son was born a week before Christmas, on December 18, 1948. No one knows, now, what time it was, or how long he fought to be born, what kind of labour his mother endured or the state of her body and mind when it was done. She would have laboured alone, with the occasional nurse dropping in, and afterwards there would have been her husband and no one else to comfort her, to tell her what an extraordinary thing she had just done. Did he? Did Michael come with flowers and smiles, to drop a kiss on her forehead, to see this small miracle, this first-born son? Peter Michael, *Panayotis Minas*, a boy who would encapsulate all his father's dreams in this new life.

That is surely what she thinks in her exhaustion, lying beneath a ticking fan in the maternity ward, as a hot tropical Christmas approaches. When white-veiled nurses bring the newborns to their mothers for breastfeeding in the row of narrow beds, she strokes her son's head with its thin fur of dark hair and knows that now it will all be better. Michael will be better, happier, gentler. He won't ever want to hurt her or abandon her in the flat again. In the face of her tiny son she can see his father, and as he sucks she can feel the kick of pleasure in her achievement: she has reproduced her love for Michael in flesh, hers and his. If there has been a hole in their relationship, some cleft that Michael's love has fallen into, this baby will fill it up. This beautiful, beautiful boy.

But in the new year Michael's disappearances resume – Saturday nights, Sundays – and his moodiness increases. She is already struggling with the strange new skin she has grown, this exhilarating but prickly mantle of motherhood. Is surprised by its tenacity: before Peter was born she had thought it would be something she could slip in and out of, this skin, that the baby would be separate from her, that somehow she would retain her singular self. Her new duality surprises her; at times it is as if the baby has not yet left her body. While she serves in the shop her eyes flick constantly to the back room where he sleeps in a rough wooden cot his father has made. Her breasts leak spontaneously if she hears him murmur or cry.

Michael has no patience for this. If the shop is busy and the baby is hungry he tells her the baby can wait. The customer comes first, she should know that. He is brusque rather than angry in front of others; sometimes she can still detect the tenderness he wooed her with. She clings to this, and to the conviction that he loves her. Of course he does; she still loves him. But Peter's cries awaken something else. Her son's utter vulnerability to harm. She feels for the first time the fierceness of this new and different love, what she might be capable of. She pulls off her apron and goes to him.

It is late on a day such as this – the baby crying and the shop stifling in its heavy blanket of humidity and heat – that Michael's anger erupts and his flat palm becomes a balled fist when he hits her. She is holding Peter, readying herself to feed him in the upstairs flat, and the punch takes her by surprise. She falls backwards onto the bed, one arm raised to protect them both, and it's a lucky fall though her head spins from the impact and her eyes sting. All she can see – all she will remember – are Michael's wild eyes, the ugly sounds he makes, the spit that flies with the barrage of Greek and speckles her cheek. She doesn't realise she has rolled herself into a ball around her son, her hands over his head, that terror has returned them both to foetal shapes. When the noise subsides and her husband has left, that is what she finds: her and Peter, wet with sweat, tucked like commas against each other. The baby is nuzzling at the cotton of her blouse.

Michael's older sister, Adriana, arrives from Sydney to see Michael's firstborn. They have moved to a small flat in a boarding house close to the shop, and Adriana casts her eye around it and tries to hide her shock; from her brother's letters she had expected something else. Something comfortable. But the flat is almost bare, there are only the necessities – a small table, chairs, an upended crate for a cupboard, an icebox. What she sees is a bad memory, the home of a pauper. Though when she looks more closely she sees a woman's touch: a doily, wildflowers in a jam tin on the table. A plate of biscuits beside the rough cups.

Now Yvonne emerges from the bedroom; another shock. She's just a girl, a dark-haired girl with nervous eyes. And a baby – Michael's son, Adriana's nephew. The reason she has come this interminable distance. He is curled against his mother's shoulder, blinking in the afternoon light. His cheeks grazed with sleep. Adriana is stung by recognition; she is instantly back in her village on Kythera, a girl herself, and it is Michael against their own mother's chest, newly born.

Instinctively, she reaches for him, and Yvonne lowers Peter into her arms, brushing his cheek with her lips. Adriana doesn't know where to look first, the tender new flesh of the baby or the face of the mother. This child her brother has married. Later, after the pleasures of arrival have subsided, and the first conversations, Adriana holds Peter and talks quietly while Yvonne prepares a meal. She sees the girl's jerky movements from table to sink to fridge, her ears cocked for the sound of her husband on the stairs, and at first this looks like eagerness. She is so young, this girl, waiting for her husband, fond.

But in the days that follow, Adriana sees she may be wrong. Her own gentle marriage has misled her. The girl's quick hands, her restless eyes: it might be love and it might be fear. Once she recognises this she watches carefully. And sees her flinch at the unexpected – Michael swatting a mosquito near her shoulder, or cursing at the baby's loud cries. Yvonne is in perpetual motion, running between the shop and the baby, the wash tub, the kitchen. And always her eyes seeking Michael's. If he is happy, dropping careless kisses on his son's head, stepping the old dances around the kitchen, Yvonne flushes and smiles. But not much. More often she shrinks a little when he walks into the room.

That is all Adriana sees until the day she leaves, when she catches something in Yvonne's eye as she kisses her, one cheek, the other. *Come again?* the girl says quietly, and Adriana has time only to smile before Michael ushers her away.

What does she know of this place she's been brought to, that she has worked in and lived in but barely seen? She works solidly from six in the morning until late most days, in the shop or within the close walls of the flat, stepping out briefly to buy milk if they've run out, or to run some errand for Michael. The errands are infrequent; he doesn't like her being out alone, even in daylight, wants to keep her close to home. In the beginning, she might have mistaken this for love.

So now when Michael is not there she takes Peter and walks the streets of the town. At these times she is often surprised by loveliness, the mountains in the soft light of early morning, or the sea along the esplanade at dusk. The ugliness and terror of her interior life at home has allowed her to forget that in this place there might be beauty and gentleness, in the sky or a human face or a flower or the lacework on a high verandah.

She begins to look for this on these walks, for signs of the lovely or just of the ordinary, pointing out to Peter the flower of the bird of paradise with its feathers and its eyes, the waving cane stalks, the sails of schooners in the harbour.

The giddy depths of green on green. On these days she misses Evelyn and her mother, the company of women. Sometimes a memory will come to her – of singing to her brothers 'The Donkey Serenade', the song she now sings to Peter, or of a Saturday afternoon at the pictures with her sister, the laughter, the flirting – and the sweetness of the old life will overwhelm her. Her chest will constrict and she'll let the tears come, all the tears she won't shed in front of Michael. In these solitary moments she empties herself out. Then she's done. The child in her arms reminds her she needs to be strong.

Summer wears on and doesn't seem to end. The humidity is a river she must walk through every day, pushing tired limbs against its tide. She frets about Peter, about keeping him cool, whether his nappies will dry. Rain tips from the sky on the hour, as if an invisible timer is at work; she has to be cunning with her trips to the makeshift washing line outside. But the moisture is cunning too, it insinuates itself, rubbing raw the skin beneath her heavy breasts, the baby's plump thighs, and painting tiny bibs or singlets bright green with mildew blossom if they're dropped and forgotten overnight.

She is always tired. The heat, the baby, the shop. The constant mindfulness of Michael's mood, his movements. And something else now that she is barely aware of: she is on the brink of malnutrition. Michael takes all the money in the till when he leaves on Saturday night for his forays to the gambling tables, and he is often away until Monday. She is left with the few remaining groceries in the cupboard, no fresh milk or meat, nothing she can cook. There is, at any rate, little time to cook, in between serving and cleaning in the shop, and seeing to Peter, as well as the usual round of domestic jobs.

Peter, at least, is thriving. At three months he is lively and happy, though his eyes are watchful, wary. She looks on with a kind of greedy pleasure as his limbs grow strong and sturdy, his skin clear and fragrant as a ripe peach. Her own skin, she notes, has lost the glow it had a year ago, has become sallow, her eyes dull. She has been told this is what happens to breastfeeding mothers who 'don't look after themselves' – the baby becomes a parasite, extracting any available goodness through her breast milk. Only the mother suffers. This doesn't bother her; beneath the weariness she is resilient and at times she can still feel it, a young woman's strength in her legs and arms and even in her spirit. It is Peter, she decides, who both takes her strength and gives it back to her.

But just as summer begins to release its tight grip, she discovers her body has betrayed her. She is pregnant again. For months she refuses to believe it, hiding the nausea and vomiting from Michael, appalled at her own reaction. This is an innocent baby she is denying, just a finger of flesh, hers and his, but still she can't rouse any joy within herself, not even the uncertain mix of exhilaration and fear she felt with Peter. For the first time she sees the changes the past year has wrought in her, a bleakness and resignation and regret. These changes, and not the new pregnancy, make her afraid.

Is it this, her tangible fear and uncertainty, that Michael senses the night he comes home from the gambling tables in Innisfail and begins to abuse her for not cooking him a meal? His anger is palpable: if she reaches a hand towards him it will sting her, she suspects, like an exposed electric current. By now she knows this fury means he has lost this weekend, probably their whole takings. The thought adds a layer of bitterness to her mixed emotions. It is her money as much as his, she has worked for it. She won't say it though she wants to, wants to ask how she could know what time he'd choose to walk in the door, and besides, what is there to cook?

She opens her mouth to protest – stupid, stupid – but before she can finish a sentence he is upon her, shaking her, shouting; amongst the barrage of foreign words she hears obscenities in English – *whore*, *bitch*, *filthy*. And now he is shoving, his hands against her shoulders, and her body is too weak to resist. As she stumbles back, one foot finds air where the floor should be, and she is suddenly falling. The steps are narrow and steep: hips and elbows and knees smack against wood. That might be the worst of it, but as her body comes to rest at the last step there is a loud cracking sound; she has only seconds for her eyes and head to register the cupboard hurtling towards her.

Until now she has been blaming herself for his anger, his neglect. Something in her must be lacking. Even as she crouches on the cold floor of the washroom that night, dazed and shuddering through the pain of miscarriage, she thinks: *I should have wanted this child more.* Everything is quiet except her breathing; Michael and his rage are subdued by night and exhaustion. Asleep, he and Peter share the innocence of all young boys. But there on the dark floor her own innocence is leaking away. When she finally expels the tiny lifeless foetus she sees the doll–like creature is another boy.

It takes only days, and the horror of hospital, where the shreds of the pregnancy are sucked from her, for self–reproach to wane and fear and anger to grow. She can't bear to think how it might have gone had Peter been in her arms when she fell, or to think of Michael's eyes as he pushed her. She wonders fleetingly what else he is capable of. Remembers her mother's words: *You make your bed, you lie in it; your place is with your husband; don't come running home after every argument.* And then: *unless he hits you.*

But Michael is all sorrow and regret, a small boy wheedling around her. He swears he will never hit her again. Holds her gently, cooing the pet name he'd once used for her – *koukla* – all that time ago. She pulls away and tells him she wants to go home.

She is surprised when he doesn't argue. Perhaps he doesn't understand she is leaving, because he says *Yes, take a holiday, see your family.* Or perhaps, by then, he is already so far gone that all he can see are the cards, the dice, the overpowering need to win. Thinking: *We'll be rich by the time she gets back. All the numbers, all the aces.*

Perhaps he doesn't see what is already lost. He buys her a ticket on the Brisbane train.

In the photograph, they are standing on a Cairns street –
Michael, my mother, and Michael's sister, Adriana – the façades
of shops in the background, the feathery top of a palm tree.
Michael is between the women, his arms around their waists.
At first glance, it's a casual family snap: the two women, sister
and wife, in the man's affectionate embrace. A sunny day, a
visitor from afar, a camera to record it. But of course, the photo
can never be just that to me, and these days, after hours of
scrutiny, I can't see how it could be just that to anyone. No
one, surely, could miss or ignore what this photo exposes. Not
just the differences in the demeanour of its subjects, in the
expression on their faces, but in what their bodies say.

Adriana looks matronly in her belted dress and comfortable
shoes, her hair pulled back from a smile you might describe
as gentle, a little restrained. Her right foot is in front of her
left, allowing the angle of her body towards her brother's.
Though the resemblance to Michael is clear, it's difficult to
tell how old she is. Her style of dress tells us she's a different
generation from her sister-in-law, or perhaps she sees herself

that way. She looks at the camera and she might be calm and she might be tentative, the quieter female sibling next to the exuberant male one.

Michael, in the middle – the centre of attention – faces the camera squarely in his white shirt and tie and pin-striped coat. His trousers are too long, but even so they reveal the scalloped leather of his fancy shoes. I'd always imagined him as big and bulked with muscle, so when I first see this picture I'm shocked at his size. He's small. Just a shade taller than my mother. He doesn't look particularly strong, either, or prepossessing in the way I'd assumed.

He's wearing a hat pushed back from his forehead, so we can clearly see the face Yvonne was transfixed by just two years before. I search it for beauty, for the allure my aunts have spoken of. *He was* very *good-looking*, they've always said, arching their brows. But all I can see is artifice and bluff. Even here, frozen in time, he is all confidence and swagger. There's not a hint of reticence in his eyes and mouth, in his practised look. It was this confidence, I suppose, the ease he exuded, that gave him his magnetism – especially to an uncertain girl. I can concede that magnetism, an echo of the dark, exotic film stars she admired – but he looks to me more pretty than handsome. It might be the grin he's wearing, a grin to mock the camera, to mock this whole situation, and perhaps us, these decades later, trying to peer into it to see.

And then there's my mother. She looks older than eighteen, the age she was when the picture was taken, in the way people often do in photos from the era of black and white, shade and shadow. She wears a dress of some dark, gauzy fabric with a tie at the waist, and her hair falls in waves just above her shoulders. Unlike Adriana, her feet are planted firmly, perhaps eight inches apart, in a stance that might be for balance or might be a refusal: her body will not be twisted around against Michael's. She is intent on facing ahead.

But that isn't what disturbs and confronts me about this photo, or not exactly. It is the look on her face. Her lips are turned down and slightly apart, her forehead is creased; there isn't even the pretence of a smile. She looks appalled by something, hunted, helpless. It is almost as if, staring into the lens of the camera, she can see the events of the next two years. She looks, I think, already damaged by what her life has been and what she fears it will become.

I examine this photo again and again. Somewhere in its grainy texture there must be some clue, some portal I can pass through to stand right there, next to them, so I can understand what she was feeling, her connection with this man, what brought them to this point in their lives together. I search it for emotion and truth, something in their eyes or lips that might reveal what is real, not shrugged on for the camera.

I try to imagine Michael as the charming, smooth-talking, charismatic man she fell in love with. I try to look at him as if I don't know anything about him. What would I read in his face? That jaunty pose, cocky, you might think he was a bit of a lair. That's all. I give up this game pretty quickly because I can't even pretend to be objective. There's too much I already know. This is the trick photography plays on us down through the years: the image, trapped in time, becomes overlaid with all that follows in its wake; we can't just look at a face from sixty years ago without imbuing it with all the knowledge we've garnered since then about the person or their life. So perhaps I project onto this photograph everything I know now about Michael and my mother, the easy cruelties, all the fears that proved well founded, the nightmares that came true. Without that knowledge, perhaps I could look at them and suppose my mother was just unhappy that day, homesick, tired. She never did like having her photograph taken, for as long as I can remember.

But I can't un-know what I know. And even if I remember the ageing effect of photography and my familiarity with the image, still I am worried by my mother's youth and the wretchedness in her face, and it takes me a long time to see why. It's the contrast with the other two, Michael and his sister, who smile openly and calmly out at me, their bodies relaxed while hers is rigid, their eyes untroubled. *Untroubled* is not a word anyone would use about Yvonne's eyes here – not me, not a stranger coming to this picture with no knowledge of her life outside the photo's edges.

In the end, though, none of that really matters, because I can't dismiss the echo of that look in expressions she wore, all through my childhood and later – not always, but often. I can close my eyes and see it now, a deep despondence, a preoccupation with old misery. As children we see it but can't decipher it, but now I can only wonder at the act of will – repeated every day of her adult life – that enabled her to break through that facial expression at all, to banish the preoccupying thought, to be – or to look – happy. *She was always so strong*, her sisters said about her, right throughout her life, and it's true. She *was* strong. And she learned to disguise heartbreak early, to subsume it in work, in hard, soul-cleansing work. But her face in that photograph hints at how much she hid, then and for the rest of her life, and how much it cost her.

The house at Cannon Hill is as cramped as ever, and made smaller by the recent birth of her mother's seventh and last child. Yvonne and Peter share a narrow room at the back of the house with the ice-chest; there is nowhere else. For her younger siblings their return is a treat: they've missed Mimi, and Peter is, at six months old, robust enough to play with. Their own mother is tired and constantly distracted by Wendy, their new baby sister, who can't even roll over yet. Ann, one of the six and a half year old twins, quickly adopts Peter as her own. She spends hours with him on a rug in the kitchen; is horrified, as she holds him on a chair one day, to feel him wriggle free and slip onto the wooden floor. What is worse is that Mimi berates her, even though Peter is more shocked than hurt and doesn't cry for long. Ann doesn't know why her big sister is so distressed.

Within a week she has casual work at The Palms, a couple of days here and there, enough to earn her keep at home. Evelyn helps to care for Peter on her days off from her own waitressing job at Rowes Arcade in Edward Street. Sometimes she dresses him up and takes him to town on the Black and White bus. They visit his mother at The Palms and then Evelyn shows him off to her girlfriends at Rowes. They fuss around him, make him laugh. Evelyn loves these trips to town: people admire the chubby-faced boy in his winter beret and blue shoes, they assume he is hers. Peter sits quietly on her hip or forearm as she strolls the length of Queen Street, his dark eyes flicking solemnly over buildings and faces and cars.

Then one day, without warning, Michael is on the doorstep, smiling his old smile. The small children crowd around him, calling *Mimi! Guess who's here!* They like Michael, they remember his playfulness, his ability to make their sister laugh. They haven't seen her laugh for a while.

He is installed at the table with tea and Peter on his lap while extra vegetables are hastily picked and added to the stew. Mimi keeps her eyes averted and low. Over dinner Michael looks at Veronica and winks; he is going to buy her daughter a house of her own, he announces. She won't have to put up with cramped boarding houses or flats again. But Veronica suspects something about the bruises on Mimi's arms, old bruises the colour of nicotine. Keeps telling her she's 'all skin and bone'. But: *He was rough with me* is all she has said, to explain the marks and her sudden arrival.

So Veronica ignores Michael's wink, but if she'd looked at Mimi, as Evelyn does, she would have seen the struggle in her eyes. In the kitchen after dinner Veronica hisses at her: *You be careful young lady*, and she's too loud as usual and Mimi tells her to shush.

Later, in the dark of the tiny back room, Michael proffers his open wallet. It is full of pound notes. Enough for an aeroplane ride to Cairns – no endless, jarring train – and she will have her house. A garden too. New clothes. *You are my wife*, he tells her. *Koukla mou*. His voice is syrupy, his hands gentle, insistent. He is, in these moments, the man she fell in love with. Optimism and longing – for him, for the life that is surely waiting for them – begin to overtake fear and resentment. She wants to believe it is still possible, that the early promise of that life will come true. That her impulsive marriage wasn't stupid after all, that *she* isn't stupid. The over-crowded house here and its thin, close walls remind her that no one's life is easy now, that there are others caught up in her decisions. When it comes down to it she feels there isn't much choice at all.

Within a week they are gone. The day they depart, Ann watches the sky from the backyard at Cannon Hill, bereft. Her brothers sit on the steps, cupping their chins. A plane finally rumbles across the sky and, convinced it's hers, they all jump up and down and wave and cry. *Mimi*, they sob, *Mimi!* As if she can hear them, as if the plane, becoming smaller, becoming invisible, will soon cease to exist. As if Mimi is gone for good.

There will be no house. The money he showed off in Brisbane was won at poker and is soon lost the same way. Michael spends more and more time at the tables and with SP bookies at the local hotels, anywhere he might trade a pound for a hundred, a thousand for five thousand. Still his losses outnumber his wins, week to week – though even a small win will usually guarantee her some peaceful days, some civility – even tenderness – from him. So she surrenders to the part of herself that still loves him, the part that believes it's all up to her to make it good. That she can. So she allows herself to trust him a little, to believe his overblown promises, to be seduced by his boasts. *Don't worry, you worry too much. We will be rich, soon enough.* Despite herself she still finds him attractive, he can still fill her with longing. It is, she supposes, a kind of enchantment, a kind of spell. But it is also her nature: she has somehow retained the shreds of her optimism, her readiness to forgive. Her readiness to see the best in people, to believe them. The bigger part of her is not even awake yet. Only catastrophe can shake that out of her.

Her trust breaks one morning in October. In the previous weeks he had begun once more to raise his hand to her, to look at her with malice and disdain, and her faith evaporates. She is surprised at her lack of surprise. Her life begins again to take on the qualities of a silent horror movie played over and over. She watches herself, fascinated, dismayed.

She is more fearful than ever of his temper now, not only because she knows its dimensions but because she can no longer deny the insistent evidence: she is, once again, pregnant. She knows precisely when this baby was conceived, in the first month after their return. There has been no possibility since. He has, she knows, been visiting the girls in Grafton Street, where every second shopfront is a brothel. She has overheard the asides when his friends are in the café, seen their furtive glances in her direction, but more than that, she can smell it on him, the briny, sweet-and-sour odour of sex.

He confirms it this October morning when she tells him she needs milk, she needs food, the cupboards are empty, the baby needs fruit. She watches fury ignite in his eyes, he tells her to *shut up*, and as she opens her mouth he slaps her. Hard. Once more she is outside herself, watching; she thinks: it sounds like a loud kiss. Her face stings. It shocks the words from her: *You've got money for girls*, and her voice is icy with hate. He makes a grab at her; she stumbles and falls and her cotton dress rides up to her thighs. He stands over her then, leering. *They're worth it*, he tells her coldly, and she feels a gob of spit hit her flesh.

That morning paints an indelible line between them. She feels something shift in herself: it's as if her heart has slipped sideways. It frightens her, this feeling, but it's accompanied by a flush of strength, a reminder of who she was before him – someone capable, strong. It isn't that she's stopped loving him – she hasn't. This fact surprises and shames her. How can she love a man who humiliates her, who finds her loathsome? But love is not an emotion she can switch off at will. What she has lost is, she realises, more important: respect. For herself – though that has been happening for months – and now she knows she has lost any vestiges of respect she once had for him.

Michael too seems to have let something go. As his gambling losses mount he begins to abandon any restraint he might have used. It is, she thinks as she scours the flat for something to quell her hunger, as if something has broken in him, something essentially human. Whenever he comes at her with bulging eyes and raised hands, she sees it clearly and terrifyingly. Whatever is lost in him is something he refuses now to identify in her. To him, she is less than human too.

She has nothing and knows no one, lost in her own life. She wouldn't tell at any rate, especially not her parents. Fear and shame keep her silent, despite everything. Despite the beatings, despite Peter and the unborn child she is determined to protect this time, the child Michael is unaware she is carrying. Some small shred of self-preservation has triumphed in her and she has not told him. Physically there is nothing to hide: she is so thin the pregnancy is not apparent, not to Michael, not to anyone. She knows instinctively it is better this way, that the news will unleash some other, unnamed anger in him. So she hugs the knowledge to herself, a tiny treasure that is hers alone. She asks the woman in the next flat if she can borrow some milk and bread, and they each pretend she's just run out of both until Michael comes home.

In the end the camel's back is broken by a thumb. A bone, thin as a kitten's, that doesn't quite snap as he grabs her hand

and bends the fingers back, cruel, intent. He is standing so close that she sees the muscle twitch in his cheek, his lips stretch across his teeth. He is putting effort into this. He wants to hear the crack of the bone breaking. But this is where her remaining strength is stored, in her hands. She twists away from him, blinking back the pain.

Later, in the kitchen, she rips an old handkerchief into strips for a bandage. It is Christmas week. On a shelf in front of her are three cards, two with a blue-clad baby and a glittery number one, another with fir trees weighed down with snow. Her boy's first birthday, Christmas: for everyone else they mean celebration and joy. Only she knows their emptiness, only she knows they are brittle and fake, without meaning. She looks at the cards every day and it is as if someone has concocted her life in sugary jingles and put it on display. With her good hand she reaches over and sweeps them to the floor.

She has become so estranged from kindness. Sitting on the back steps that night, after Peter is asleep and Michael has left, she wraps her arms around her knees and leans her cheek there. Her thumb throbs but her eyes are dry; there is nothing left to cry for.

This is how it seems to the woman in the flat next door, this is what she sees in the sickly yellow light from her kitchen window: a pale, limp figure of defeat. A mere outline of a girl. She is thin and weak and the woman thinks of paper, brittle, transparent. She could be nudged off the stairs by someone's hot breath, or a shout.

She would like to offer something. But has no right, and no responsibility. So she just calls from her doorway, not loud, not soft, *Hot enough for you love?* and the girl lifts her head. Her eyes are blank but she pushes a half-smile out into the night. Nods. Absently strokes a bandaged thumb, up and down. *Hmm*, she says. That's all. *Yes.* The woman next door follows the girl's eyes, that half-smile. But it's only the cool night sky of the tropics, a spatter of stars. And the crescent moon grinning.

Who sees her, who hears? Everyone does, everyone: her face becoming a gargoyle, her voice thinning. The look and sound of misery are the same in all places, in all languages. Each one who sees and hears is afraid of his or her own capacities and incapacities, is angry with her for reminding them. This is what she is guilty of, this mirroring, that and her own complicity in it all. She is still there, nothing changes. She herself is to blame.

The woman next door has seen and heard. She is confronted, afraid not just of Michael but of the girl, because in her suffering, in her role as the receiver and bearer of pain, she has become other. The woman next door, like everyone else, has seen the slight body, the shadowed face, and sees everything she herself isn't but could be. But it is all pushed down, subterranean, it barely breaks the surface – her own half-realised desire to keep seeing, to be the watcher. To keep hearing through the wall, to be the witness. If she is the witness, she is not the victim.

But this night, the night the woman sees her on the steps, seems to make her more than witness, diminishes the distance between their bodies. Perhaps it is their voices, a question, a reply, all the things they leave unspoken. A kind of tenderness opens up beneath the words. Something female, something motherly, something human. A kind of goodness.

So she does what she can do. She begins to look at the girl differently – at her face, her movements, her mail – as a hunter looks for signs. And is soon rewarded: the day before Christmas, in the batch of letters in the hallway, an envelope with a return name and address. Inside, a card, *Happy Christmas, love from Mum and Dad*, and a pound note. Relief courses through her: the girl has parents. She copies the address, re-seals the envelope with its precious pound, slips it under her door. Later, she will write a careful note and send it to V.C. and E.H. Ball at Bomberry Street, Cannon Hill, Brisbane.

When Veronica pulls the letter from her mailbox in early January, she frowns over the handwriting as she tucks her finger beneath the flap of the envelope, and gives a little cry that brings old Eliza to her side. From the brief sentences on thin airmail paper they will both remember one line, and repeat it to each other over and over, for years. *Get your daughter out of here, before he kills her.*

No point in the police. No need to talk or tell. No one has the power, or the money. The wherewithal. Least of all Veronica. Ham-tied by children, an empty purse, frustration. She *told* her. So it is Eliza, Old Gran, who acts. She knows the delicacy that is needed, the force: both must match Michael's. She buys a one-way train ticket, Cairns to Brisbane, puts it in an innocent envelope and posts it to her granddaughter. The note is as eloquent as the one that prompted it: *Get out. Come Home. Love, Gran.*

I have three photographs of Cairns railway station in the late 1940s: a two-storey building with cross-timbered balcony rails and the stark round face of a railway clock. A line of cars is parked tail-in along the front, all running boards and jutting bonnets and spoked wheels. The third photo, faded, shadowy, gives me a partial glimpse of the platform. It is narrow and open, with small round flowerbeds and thin light-poles; you can see the curved roofs of train carriages, and coal bunkers in the background.

But I am looking for the thin figure of a woman with a baby clutched to her side. I am trying to make out the shape of her, the set of her shoulders, her walk. The kind of shoes she had on. She had fine-shaped ankles, beautiful, all her life. That morning sixty years ago they carried her, the baby, a suitcase, the weight of all her fear and courage, along this strip of sunlit platform, this strip of bitumen that might be a line drawn between her two lives. Between her two selves: the one naive and hopeful, the other bitter and self-condemning, grieving, unable to forgive herself or the world for the loss of her child. I have spent much of my life trying to impress the one, and now I am trying to understand the other.

Everything about the train is a taunt, a jibe, an accusation – its noise, its power, its forward motion. The windows flash endless images at her, mile after mile: Peter, Peter, Peter. Somewhere after Townsville, exhaustion wins and she slides into sleep. Wakes hours later to shame and dread, as if she has slept through her watch. As if she has betrayed him with these brief hours of unconsciousness. All the hours to Brisbane she tries to stay vigilant, invoking magic of any kind to stay awake, but she has forgotten what the body knows. What *her* body knows: it needs rest. In between the stops, the railway tea and scones and fish dinners she has no money for, sleep claims her again. Until she opens her eyes to the rusted tin roofs of Brisbane's suburbs, of Virginia and Banyo and Wooloowin, the clock tower of the City Hall in the distance, and she knows she is home.

The colours of her homecoming are red and black. This is Ann's memory, vivid, frightening: her sister's hair, too straight, too black, her red dress too red for the sadness all around her as she stumbles from the train, alone. No baby. Ann looks past Mimi to the carriage door, as if Peter might appear with one of the other passengers smiling with the relief of arrival. But there is no Peter, only Mimi who is not smiling, who subsides against their mother and sobs. Ann can hardly bear to listen to the noise that she can only think of as thin, because that is what her sister is, everything about her is thin, her face, her arms, even her lips. When she stops crying she presses them tightly together, as if she is afraid of what might happen if she opens those lips again. She kisses everyone thinly. Then they take her home. But she's not there long; the next day they take her to see a doctor and she doesn't come back.

She lies in a hospital bed and feels her future draining into her past. She is helpless before it; has become a mere onlooker, a witness to her own life, the high steel bed at once her prison and her grandstand. The word of the doctors binds her: she must lie here if she wants this baby inside her to survive, if she herself wants to survive. There are nights, edged hard with grief, with a loathing for her own traitorous flesh, when she would choose not to live. No one else seems to see the bargain that's been made: the new baby for the one lost. Every day she lies here motionless, saving this baby's life, is another day she isn't saving Peter. Fighting for him. By obeying the doctors, she is disobeying her own heart.

She isn't surprised when her daughter is born early and tiny at the end of March, 1950; a female replica of her son, with a shock of dark hair. Yvonne's struggling kidneys keep them both in hospital for another month, but there is no hurry to get home. There is no home, no husband, no little boy, nothing, despite the wedding band on her finger, despite the changes to her name, her body, to virtually every aspect of her life.

She names the baby Sharon Elaine. Sharon for the rose. Elaine for no one we know about. But here is my guess: she has anglicised the Greek name *Elena*. This is the name she called Sharon, playfully, all her life. *Elaina*. A pet name. A name to stamp a child with a history, an oblique but insistent connection with her father. With her brother. It's not so strange. The marriage is over, that much is clear, but still she is mourning the potential of it, of all her dreams. Here is a new child, flesh of their flesh, who should have been part of the life they might have had. So perhaps the name is a kind of talisman, for Sharon, for herself. A lure that will bring Peter back.

We are all born into some quality of air, of mood, of atmosphere. A kind of receiving blanket of emotion: joy, regret, fear, celebration. This child has been born to a mother already grieving the things she cannot give her: a father, a brother, a home. It is just fifteen months since Peter's birth – a day still fresh in her mind. But this time there is no joy in seeing the father in the child, the fusing of beloved flesh with her own. Did she feel the triumph she felt at Peter's birth, the elation that accompanies exhaustion? The achievement of it?

Thirty years later, after the birth of my own second child, there was a moment when she might have said. We were in her kitchen, my mother and I, drinking tea while my baby son slept nearby in his Moses basket and the radio played softly behind us. I don't remember the conversation, only a pause as the voice of Roberta Flack began to drift around us: 'The First Time Ever I Saw Your Face'. That other-worldly sound, and then my mother, telling me that whenever she heard this song she thought of each one of her children, and the moment we were born. As she spoke she looked at me with that half-smile of hers, and I was startled for a moment, because it felt like a confession, or a gift, which might be the same thing. A glimpse of the woman beneath the layers of armour, one sentence from a forbidden book.

But there had been so many things forbidden, so many things unsaid. If she was offering me something then, I was too inured to silence to take it up. We held that moment between us until she lowered her eyes and we both let it go. The book closed. I looked down at my son. The euphoria of his birth still washed through my blood, I could smell it in my pores, in the webbed air between his body and mine. How could I possibly understand fully what she said to me that day? I was struck dumb by love, by possession. I didn't know if she was talking about joy or loss, and I couldn't ask. Even now, I can only guess how she felt, not just then but alone in her hospital bed back in 1950, pushing aside the food she was meant to eat and grow strong on, tipping warm eggnogs down the sink. This is what I think: she looked down at her second child, just as I looked at mine, but she'd been assailed by a sense of utter aloneness, of fear. The air my sister was born into, I see now, was heavy with ambivalence and with doubt.

She takes Sharon back to the only home she knows, the house at Cannon Hill. To the little room with the ice-chest at the back, to the noisy routine of her parents and her younger siblings. She is nineteen years old. A new mother again with a new baby, but waking each morning to the absence of the other. Each morning she lies there in her narrow bed, summoning the strength to get up, to face the long minutes and hours without him.

She can see Peter in the new baby's face, hear him in her cry. She clasps Sharon to her, finds it difficult, initially, to leave her for even an hour. If she does she is anxious until the baby is once more in her arms. At night she dreams of drowning in a calm sea, of surfacing briefly to scream at those on shore, but her cries are soundless. She has no voice. The water pulls her down and still she struggles upwards, flailing. She wakes before the drowning, before the inevitable. But still feels powerlessness in every part of her. For the rest of her life she will be frightened by the prospect of immersion, will not swim in the sea or a backyard pool or even the shallows of a sluggish creek.

Blindly, she claws around for ways to get her son back. Thinks of catching a train to Sydney, surely Adriana will help. Scribbles notes to Michael, full of demands, then screws them up, bitter origami, and drops them in a bin. There is no sense, she remembers, in writing letters to a man who can't read. Futility grows with every day.

So getting out of bed in those early months might be the easy part, because it means night and all its demons are gone and she can enter the day once more, the busy, active day. She has another child to feed and care for and besides, she has to rebuild her strength, recover herself. *Recover herself.* It's true that she feels something essential, something innate, has been taken, some vital part that needs to be restored before she can breathe properly again. Her whole body feels unreliable. She gets to the end of each day and it feels like a miracle, at times: her heart has kept beating, her body stayed upright, all the way through that succession of hours. Each one of them is a quicksand of bottomless grief and yes, it is miraculous that she manages to step around them. Some days the quicksand looks like a mercy; she wants to enter it, and sink.

Despite the cramped conditions they all try to help, to get along. But Ann is distressed and confused. Mimi is back but Peter is gone. She remembers a roly-poly baby, a big live doll who squirmed in her arms and laughed when she said *boo!* and watched them from a rug on the floor as they ate their dinner. She would be chipped for talking to him with her mouth full, but she didn't care. She loved him. In his short stay the year before he'd claimed a chunk of her loyal child's heart. She would never forget him. But it seems to her that everyone else, her mother and father, Mimi, Evelyn, is almost choking now on his name. It is stuck in their throats and won't come out.

At first she asks about him quietly, plaintively. *Where's Peter?* There would be no answer, they would divert her with an errand – *help your sister with her shoes, Annie, turn the wireless down* – or a sudden need to attend to one of the boys. Finally, after her second or third query one day: *Shh!* her mother hisses over her shoulder from the laundry tub. *Don't talk about it. You'll upset your sister.*

But Ann can see it is already too late for that. Her sister's face says so every day. Every day her face looks broken somehow, empty, though she has a new baby now who sleeps where Peter once slept. The new baby is nice, and she looks like Peter, but she isn't Peter. Ann is afraid this baby might disappear too, that Mimi might go away again. She watches her. Stays close to her, leaning over her shoulder as she breastfeeds Sharon, tagging along to the shop. She hears and stores up snatches of conversation, words not meant for her ears, like *bastard*, like *heartbroken*. She can only think of her own heartbeat, stopping, breaking. Ann, watching Mimi for clues, becomes a quiet witness to her sister's sorrow.

The man in the public trustee's office listens while she tells him how it was. What she wants. He's a middle-aged man in a white shirt and sleeves rolled up, his tie a bland brown in a Windsor knot. She's comforted by his eyes – they creased when he smiled a hello – but now, as she speaks, they betray nothing. He leans into his high-backed chair, moves a pencil from one hand to the other. His gaze drops to the pencil occasionally, as if it is fascinating, or perhaps it's his knuckles. They sprout lively dark hairs. *My son.* In front of him a blotter, pen and ink and notebook cut by a knife-edge of light from the window. She stops, her own eyes drop to the desk, silky oak like the old bed she sleeps in at home with her daughter. The room holds its breath.

I want my son back.

The man looks up from his pencil. Holds it between two index fingers, end to end.

Yes, he says.

Her face is on fire. She has tried for dignity, but the words give her away, words no wife should have to utter. No one has heard them before, these words, this story, not like this. Only her sister Evelyn. Shame flames in her cheeks. But then she remembers why she's here.

I want my son back. Her voice her own now, her chin up and the flame shifts to her eyes.

The man waits a beat and throws out his line. *We can get him back.* Leans forward then, flips the pencil onto the desk between them. Another beat. *But they'll come and get him again. You know that, don't you?*

She looks at his face, gauging. Waits.

And then we'll find him and bring him back, and then they'll find him . . . and so on.

The shaft of sunlight is projecting a broken movie reel now, the same scene over and over, forward and reverse: Michael yanks Peter out of her arms, puts him back, yanks him out, puts him back. She sits in the chair opposite the man in the white shirt and tries not to hate him. Her body is rigid, her hands clasping her elbows. Holding herself.

The man says: *He'll spend the rest of his childhood being pinched out of backyards.* Then: *Besides, after what his father's done to keep him, he'll be treated like a prince. He'll be a doctor or a lawyer.* He cocks his head. *Or the child of an unmarried waitress. Is that the kind of life you want for him?*

The question hangs in the air. She feels chastened, as she is meant to. This shameful question is being asked of hundreds of young women around the country then, in these years of unwed mothers, non-existent contraception and powerless young women. In these years of rampant theft: the children of Indigenous families snatched from their mothers, the children of the poor seized and charged with *neglect* – as if they are wilfully, stubbornly, shamelessly poor – and thrown into children's homes; the babies of unmarried women forcibly adopted out; those of disadvantaged British parents taken from their parents and brought alone to institutions in remote parts of Australia. Each family was told: *Your child will have a better life.*

So in a sense the question my mother was asked that day was rhetorical. The man might have said, *If you care about him, if you're a good mother, you'll leave him alone. You'll drop this now.* But he doesn't. He leaves it at that: *Is that the kind of life you want for him?* and stands, telling her to think about it, come back if she wants to. Dismissing her.

She walks out into broad sunshine and her body aches with the ordinariness of the day, with the plainness of loss. It is all around her; in the eyes of shattered men and grieving women who, just five years after the end of the war, present a stoic face to the world. There is always someone worse off. *Don't forget how lucky you are*, she would say to us all much later, if we lamented our shortcomings or the things we didn't have. We tried to believe it, just as she did that day in 1951, reminding herself of greater losses, bigger sacrifices, of pain that eclipsed her own. She is, in the scheme of things – war and death and illness, a kind of mass bereavement – *lucky.*

Still, she stands there outside the lawyer's office and her hands open and close, open and close, as if she is on a train instead of a main street, as if her baby is being wrenched from them all over again.

As soon as she can she goes back to the work she knows – waitressing in cafés and milkbars, serving in a cake shop, sewing. The lawyer was right: she has left Cairns with nothing; her two years of sweatshop labour for Michael have delivered her into poverty, with less materially than she has ever had. Her parents cannot support her; there is no help from government and little from the community. She doesn't expect any. Veronica looks after Sharon, and Mimi pays for that as well as for their board and keep. It means there are two little girls under two vying for attention in the house, along with the twins, who are just eight. But Ernest's job as a wards-man and gardener at a northside hospital barely pays the bills, even with Evelyn and the older boys, Ernie and Geoffrey, paying board from their wages too. So minding Sharon means money coming into the house, and money is what they need most of all.

Somewhere over the next two years, her grief blossoms out of its fist of pure pain and into something that is sinuous and usable. It isn't conscious. The despair begins to take on different qualities, become something else. Part of her has been burned in a crucible and emerged tougher, harder. She regards the world differently, the people in it. Sees she isn't entirely without power after all: there might be ways to make something from what she's lost. As she sits at her sewing machine, her foot rhythmic on the treadle, she thinks that mistakes can, perhaps, be unpicked like stitches. The cloth might be cut to suit.

It happens something like this: as she reaches twenty-one, she is still a dark beauty, though her eyes are guarded and her air unattainable. Men are drawn to her, moths to a quiet flame. They watch her at work, on the tram, in the street, and she knows they watch her. After the pain and humiliation of Michael, there is satisfaction in this, even triumph: she *knows* she is beautiful. She has abandoned all fear of conceit, any concern she might have about arrogance or pride. She decides that, as it has brought her down in the past, this beauty, she can also use and manipulate it to her own ends. In this she has learned much from Michael. Beauty, she knows now, is a fine weapon.

She is regularly invited out by young men she meets in town and by some who knew her as a girl. She has just as regularly declined. Now she begins to accept, one after another. In one week she has three invitations; she accepts them all. And all for the same Friday night, and at the same time, seven o'clock. She tells each to meet her on a corner of the intersection of Queen Street and George. One, two, three; one corner for each. When the night arrives she pulls on a hat of her mother's, a lumpy coat, flat shoes, and stands behind a pillar on the fourth. She waits and watches.

Each man turns up and stands at his designated place, unaware of the others. She notes how carefully they've all dressed, the Brylcreemed hair, the ironed shirts. Ties too. She watches as they brush their palms across their shoulders, adjust their cufflinks, check their reflections in glass. Her heart begins to thump with the first glance at a wristwatch, the first sign of uncertainty – a shuffling of feet, a look in both directions, a frown. She smiles a grim and pretty smile as they check their watches more frequently, as the question flares in their chests, sweeps their faces. Their newly shaved cheeks. Have they mistaken the agreed time? Are they in the right place? Has she missed her bus, forgotten their date? Some of them wait for a whole hour. But usually, well before eight o'clock, they've dug their hands into their pockets and, at various intervals, wandered away.

I can't remember when she told me this story, or how old I was, or what prompted it, only a brightness that flamed in her eyes. A kind of pride and defiance, as if she was challenging me, or perhaps herself, in the telling. There was no attempt to explain it, or elaborate, and because I didn't know the context then I didn't understand. *I suppose I hated men*, she said with a shrug when I asked her why, and that was the end of it. My skin goosed with the image she'd made, the hopeful faces of the boys, the grim satisfaction on hers, but I also felt a shiver of the familiar. Something that took me a while to trace.

It came one day when I'd dropped by so that Mum could fit a dress she'd made for me. She was pinning up the sides, her hands and fingertips on my hips, smoothing the curve of fabric over my waist. We all loved this process, even as adults: our mother moving around us with pins and tape measure, her hands and eyes on our bodies, the physical intimacy we all yearned for and she couldn't often give. We'd try to make it easy for her, pretending she'd pinched us or pierced our skin, shrieking like barbarians. She'd grin through the pins pursed between her teeth and tell us to keep still.

She was nearly done with me when my sister came up the back steps. Sharon's marriage had disintegrated and she'd moved in with her girlfriend by then – the air in the house was still thick with a tangible anxiety and disapproval. Sharon leaned in and kissed our mother's cheek, said a bright hello, but there was barely a response. My sister flashed me a knowing look, and in the interminable minutes that followed – Sharon made small-talk as she put the kettle on, I made small-talk back, and Mum said next to nothing – I remembered the boys she'd left on street corners. In effect, I realised, that's what she was doing to Sharon, what she did to all of us whenever we upset or offended her, sometimes without knowing how. She would simply withdraw. There would be an icy silence, a kind of grand sulk that could last for weeks, the air around her sharp as knives. We called it *the cold winds of Siberia*, and though we can joke about it now, at the time it felt like exile from her, and from her grace. It was the worst kind of punishment.

When Michael arrives on Adriana's doorstep in Sydney she greets him with disapproving eyes. She knows; the image of Yvonne is still with her, Yvonne shrinking from him, her arms protective. Her body still full and soft from childbearing, like fruit easily bruised. The way it curled around Peter as she held him. Adriana has told her husband Spiro: *He hurts her.*

Michael spins the line anyway. She's gone/left the baby/run away with some spiv. Peter huddles in his father's arms. Adriana takes him, and Michael saunters past her and into the kitchen. Adriana talks to Peter, kissing his fists, his head. He's beautiful, beautiful. He has his mother's eyes. Before she knows it, she's agreed to help with Peter while Michael goes up to Junee to look at a café. He'll send for the boy as soon as he can. Spiro says nothing; he lets them talk and quietly slips away.

But the next day, before Michael leaves, Spiro corners him in the yard. There is a fig tree, a clothes hoist, basil and oregano in olive oil tins. A wrought-iron table and chairs beneath the fig, where friends sometimes sit with their coffee and cake. Spiro won't sit here with Michael. He stands near the flapping shirts and underwear, hesitates – some unspoken solidarity is about to be broken – but when he finally speaks it is brief and clear. *It's not right*, he says, *what you did*. Grinding the end of a cigarette into the grass with the toe of his shoe. *The boy needs his mother.* He stares into Michael's unyielding face then brushes past him. Spiro will never speak more than a handful of words to his brother-in-law again.

In autumn or early winter in 1951, Michael sends for his son. The shop is up and running and Peter, now about eighteen months old, is ushered into the care of Mrs White, of Ducker Street. I know nothing about Mrs White, or whether things might have gone differently had he gone to a different home in a different street. But I do have her letter, written in the style of the time by a woman who had perhaps not finished her schooling. From the tone of the letter she seems genuine, interested in Peter's welfare, though her interest might be heightened by a sense of responsibility or even guilt about Peter. If so it's most likely misplaced.

The letter is dated July 20, 1951 and was sent from 1 Ducker Street, Junee. *Dear Mrs Hill* (it reads) *Would you mind informing me if little Peter Prineas* (sic) *is in The Home, a patient from polio. The reason I am interested in him is because I was looking after him for nearly twelve months before he got polio and he was taken from here to Wagga Hospital for treatment, then I understand he was being sent to Camperdown Children's Hospital for further treatment, but on inquiries he has not been admitted there, so thought he may have went*

*to The Far West Home instead for treatment. I am very fond of Peter
and would like to know how he is getting along. Trusting I am not
putting you to too much trouble. Yours faithfully (Mrs) L. White*

There would have been little she could do. When Peter
arrived in Ducker Street, Australia's third and deadliest polio
epidemic was just beginning, there was no vaccine, and no one
could know who would be a target.

Now we know the polio virus flourishes amid poor hygiene –
but that it's harder than other viruses to remove from the skin
with soap and water. So it's difficult to work out how and why
Peter got sick at Ducker Street. I only know this: that some
time late in that year, or early in the next, as he runs around in
that ordinary backyard, Peter is felled by one of the century's
most virulent diseases, one that will take thousands of lives,
leave thousands paralysed and any number of others – mainly
children – disabled for life.

It happens like this: one day his legs and throat simply fail
him, leaving him prone in the dirt at the back of Mrs White's,
unable to escape the searing heat in his muscles and his lungs.
He is just two years old, so his brain can't process what the
fever and muscle cramps mean, apart from the overwhelming
feeling of being hurt. He cries, but even his voice is weak. He
can't make the pain understood, to others or to himself. His
body is all sharp, jagged sensation but he will not remember
this precisely, or the months that follow.

Instead, memory short-circuits in his young brain, storing
itself in his limbs, his muscles, waiting. But the sense of being
alone, without a face shaped in the familiar – that is different;
it will always track back to this time, when he is scooped up
once again and isolated from everything he knows, this time

in a series of hospital wards that smell of confusion and pain.

The first is inside Wagga Wagga Base Hospital, the closest to Junee that boasts an isolation ward for infectious diseases. Like the others there he is allowed no visitors, not his father, not Mrs White. So he is among strangers, amid strangeness – the whiteness of rooms and curtains and sheets, the starched clothes worn by women and men he doesn't know, the strangeness of pain and his own body. People with masked faces poke and prod him; there are terrifying injections in his back and arms. Voices – some warm and gentle, some harder, impatient – float above him. The idea of his father, his face, any notion of comfort, begin to dissolve in his baby's brain.

It is soon apparent he has the worst form of the disease – paralytic polio – though his lungs and other organs will be unaffected. Through his brain and spinal cord the virus has attacked his right leg and, to a lesser extent, his left arm. He is confined to a cot, in a steel brace in which his limbs are stretched and hot blankets are applied to his poor muscles to sooth the agonising contractions. The smell of hot, damp wool will always summon a sick feeling in him, some formless dark sensation.

He will stay in this ward until his condition is considered stable, a small, distressed boy among other distressed children, pinned by pain, unable to move. Then, perhaps a month, perhaps two, after toppling into the grass and dirt in Mrs White's garden, his world is upended again when he is deemed out of danger and moved to the Far West Children's Home in Sydney, where the long process of rehabilitation will begin.

Two things will intervene to change my mother's life: a meeting and a job, and they are linked by their setting, New Farm, the oldest of suburbs. The job looks, initially, like any other: caring for the elderly patients of a nursing home on Bowen Terrace, across the river and a long tram and bus ride from Cannon Hill. 'Clinton' is a lowset old Queensland house with wide verandahs flung out to meet the shadows of figs and camphor laurels that tower around it. Like its neighbour, 'Clareview', the wooden house is warrened with high-ceilinged rooms and passageways that have been variously adapted, first to the needs of American military officers stationed here during the war, and now to its elderly private clientele and their various physical and mental ailments. Rooms have been divided or enlarged and bathrooms added, carpets and rugs cover the hoop pine floorboards. But in its detail and furnishings there are still traces of the family home it once was, the sash windows that bring breezes off the river, the tongue-and-groove, the hand-tooled sideboards and velour couches, the piano. It has an air of weary gentility, like a once wealthy aunt who must make do with last year's coat, her dignity intact in her bearing, her old pearls.

But for Yvonne, Clinton is not, from the first day she steps tentatively across its verandah, merely that assembly of physical detail, though she instantly loves its form and grace. Clinton is Mary Sessarago, the redoubtable matron and owner, a formidable, shrewd and generous woman whom, despite a long connection that will outlive Clinton, my mother will always call 'Matron'. Mary Sessarago is ten years her senior and different from everyone Yvonne knows: well educated, well spoken and well connected. She has a presence that strikes the younger woman immediately. It is imperious, certainly; it is clear she is the boss. But watching her those first days, Yvonne sees not just her authority, her exacting standards, her upright carriage, but something she will always call 'good breeding' – a lack of discernible prejudice, an ease with people at both ends of the social strata.

My mother also sees and deeply envies Matron's knowledge not just of nursing but of art and literature and classical music – the evidence is all around, in the paintings on the walls of the house, in the silky oak of the Rosenstengel furniture, in Matron's allusions to Dickens, to Brahms. The nursing standards in the home are high and Matron is unforgiving of any lapse, but Yvonne is not afraid of that or of her. She sees that Mary Sessarago has much to teach her and over the next few years she sets about learning. Both Matron and Clinton – along with its extraordinary and changing cast of characters – will become pivotal in my mother's life. They will alter her view of herself and the world, and give her once more a fledgling sense of worth.

She finds she has a natural affinity with the work. It may be born of her early care and nurturing of her siblings, her knowledge of the rhythms and demands of the everyday, her lack of fear of the human body and its functions and failures. She quickly learns the basic manual skills of nursing, the 'obs' – checking blood pressure, temperature and pulse – dressing wounds, lifting and bathing, administering medication and injections. Mary Sessarago watches: as she holds thin wrists, and dresses sores on withered limbs, as she feeds and walks and cajoles. Sees her willingness to stay late, to sit with the sick or the frightened, to scrub and tidy and talk. To close the eyes of those who have taken their last breaths, to lay them out. And she sees that Yvonne watches *her*, learning. She is not afraid of old bodies and fragile minds – not afraid of frailty, of unpredictable behaviour or capricious moods. She knows, at first, little about Yvonne's past, but from her demeanour she decides that the younger woman's empathy, especially for the old, must have grown from knowing fear and frailty herself.

Yvonne loves this work. She loves the plain white uniform she wears each day, the throb of blood in the veins of a wrist as she counts its beat, the puff of air in the sphygmo, the magic of mercury in a glass thermometer. She loves the person she becomes when she walks through Clinton's door: a person without a history, who might invent herself, a whole new version, each day. This person is competent, quick, unafraid. More important, perhaps, respected. And good. She is a nurse; she tends to the ailing. Yvonne walks the halls and rooms of the old house in this woman's skin, and starts to believe she might be real.

But the Yvonne who goes home from Clinton to Cannon Hill is still the impulsive and injured young woman, dependent on the help of her parents, her anger and shame dangerously near the surface. Everything she hides at Clinton waits for her here. One night at home, Veronica, gruff, impatient, worn down no doubt by seven children and her own forfeited dreams, finds Mimi crying on the darkened back steps of the house. Perhaps Veronica has had a bad day, perhaps she just needs her daughter to buck up, but on this night she has no sympathy to spare. *For God's sake*, she barks, *stop crying over a bloody man*, and sends her inside to bath the twins.

My mother told me this story late in her life. It was another conversation about Veronica, how hard, how short-sighted she could be. Wedged between her words and sentences, between what she said and what I heard, was Peter's disappearance, the old resentments about Veronica's role, her callous indifference, as my mother saw it. By then I knew the basic facts about Peter, about Michael, but still I knew it was dangerous and distressing territory to enter, even if led. I wanted badly to know more, to ask: *Did Veronica really mistake the grief of losing a child for the disappointment of losing a man?* But I didn't. By then I was more skilled at digging between the sentences, for hearing what was beneath.

And the thing was, Veronica *was* tough. But she wasn't callous, and I wonder now if she was simplifying her daughter's grief that night because she knew its real dimensions, knew how dangerous it could be. My mother was furious with her, of course – she recounted this and other stories about Veronica in bitter tones, her lips pursed – because all she could see was that, in her parents' house, there was no room for grieving, no allowance for loss. You had to pull yourself together, get over it, get tough. *Stop crying.*

My mother was right: there wasn't much allowance for loss. There was too much of it then, and Veronica had lost too – her brother Charlie to the war, her own youth, her husband's attention, her vision of herself as a *gay dog*, unencumbered by the endless needs of others. But she knew that loss was everywhere; no one was spared. You had to count your blessings. Her daughter had made her bed and would have to lie in it.

In the early evening of a day when she has run between patients —
a day so busy it seems to end just after it begins — she walks
to the kitchen to make tea. Stops with the kettle in her hand,
midway from stovetop to sink. The realisation like a stone in her
belly: she hasn't thought about Peter since lunch. Several hours,
two hundred minutes. She is torn between guilt and surprise.
She thinks about the advice she's been given, all well meaning
and mostly ignored. Except one piece that might, she thinks
now, have been right. *Keep busy.*

The next afternoon, when Matron's face is pinched and her
words harsh because Cook has not arrived for work, Yvonne stops
her in the corridor and looks her in the eye. *I'll do it,* she says.

You're not a cook. Mary Sessarago is already moving away.

Give me a go, Yvonne says to her back. A pause. *What else are
you going to do?*

She is not afraid of her tasks in the big, pale kitchen. They are as
familiar as her own hands. She has learned this much from her

mother and her grandmother: cooking for many is not about precision so much as good big pots and preparation. Vegetables are peeled and chopped and left to soak. Jellies made and put to set on a sill. She can go about her ward duties then, hurrying back to the kitchen to mix and bake and simmer: stews and meat loaves, skirt steak braised in gravy, custards and cakes. The dull surfaces of bench-tops and pots reflect back her gratitude for the hours that pass without the ache, without the stone inside her. So whenever Cook is ill or indisposed, Yvonne takes the extra shifts not just for the fatter pay packet but, ironically, for the respite. Her body might tire but it won't fight, will do as it's told. It's her mind and her relentless heart she needs a break from.

Sharon's memory begins here, skipping between the two poles of her mother's life: home, and Clinton. Of the early years in the house at Cannon Hill there is little. It survives in a handful of images, a pull of emotion: high back stairs and a landing, the sting of a mosquito bite, a blue pedal car. Her grandmother's face. A feeling of the air being stretched around her, thin and brittle.

The house is too small and the personalities too different. The two little girls, Sharon and Wendy (who is one year older, and her aunt), don't get along; there are grating tensions between Ernest and Veronica over money, over Sharon, the long hours of childcare. Ernest finds Sharon difficult; there is a wildness to the child, he thinks. She is loud and too adventurous – even at three she hangs from tree branches, climbs fences, tumbles around the yard until her clothes are in shreds. And she yells! Old Gran has dubbed her *Skeeta* since the night they all went running to Sharon's screams, to find the monster pursuing her was a mosquito.

Wendy is quieter. Ernest finds it easy to dote on her, his youngest and last child, taking her on outings, buying her small gifts. But he tells his eldest daughter that she must be fair: anything she buys for Sharon she must also buy for Wendy. So she does: two dresses, two dolls, two blue pedal cars. She puts them on lay-by, pays them off weekly until she can bring them home.

Veronica struggles to feed and care for them all and keep the peace. And it may be the different temperaments or it may be merely that Sharon is one too many, but when the girls' arguments turn physical and frequent it is usually Sharon who is blamed. Veronica is worn out and Ernest has lost his patience. At these times he will march to the phone box at the end of the street and make a call to Clinton. *The girls are playing up and it's too much for your mother,* he'll say. *You'll have to come home.* Grim-faced, Yvonne pulls off her apron and takes a tram and a bus to Cannon Hill. More often than not, she will pack a change of clothes for Sharon and take her daughter with her, back to Clinton.

Sharon doesn't mind; Clinton is like a second home. For her, it is all startling colour and detail, vivid. She sits at the table in the big kitchen; curls of translucent orange peel off carrots, peas pop from their pods, the white flesh of potatoes looks miraculous beneath her mother's knife. Or she plays in dappled light behind the house with another child, Matron's, who calls Yvonne *Bim Bom* and follows her around as if she is his mother too. The two children watch everything. From the yard they can see the back landing where the impossibly old people sit in the sun; their favourite is called The Mad Hatter, she's there in her multiple hats, *one, two, three, four* and then they lose count.

Then there are the night shifts: her mother clutches her hand and a torch, and they follow its beam down the dark corridors and into each room, checking, listening. Sharon is caught between the thrill and the terror of it, the creaks and moans of the old house, her certainty that The Mad Hatter will materialise in the blackness, laughing her terrible laugh.

If Yvonne's work is long and hard, if there are problems at home and heaviness weighs inside her, still she has the satisfaction of work well done and the consolation of friends. Women who know her and love her, who would understand and forgive, if that was needed, the things she cannot understand or forgive about herself. Evelyn – though she is married now and out of reach on a vast cattle property in western Queensland – has always known her best. But their friends Shirley and Valerie now see and hear what Evelyn doesn't. It was Shirley, now Evelyn's high-spirited, indomitable sister-in-law, who introduced Yvonne to Clinton. And it is Val, whose own spirit is barely diminished by an alcoholic husband who disappears with the food money, who steps in to help with Sharon.

If there is trouble at Cannon Hill or emergencies at Clinton, Val takes Sharon off to play with her own two, perhaps to stay a few nights. Sometimes, when Yvonne arrives to collect her, Val is heating soup for dinner on the flame of the kerosene heater because the gas has been cut off. *Bloody Charlie*, Val will say, and then cheer them both up with a joke.

Have you ever thought about qualifying, Yvonne? As a nurse. Mary Sessarago says it to the papers she is peering at on the green leather of the desk.

Yvonne is standing almost at attention, a little breathless at the summons. This may account for her confusion. The question is simple enough, after all, but she doesn't know how to answer. She blurts: *What do you mean, Matron?*

Matron's words are clipped, her diction sharp, as always. *You're a natural, Yvonne. You should enrol to study. You could go far.*

Yvonne tries to read Matron's eyes but her head is still tilted; she can't see them. *That would cost money*, she says to the crown of Matron's head. *And there's Sharon. And* – a pause – *I didn't finish school.* There, she's said it. To the most educated woman she knows.

I'll put you through. And the schooling won't be a problem. Matron finally looks up. The set of her face, her firm lips, the voice, are compelling. Most people find it hard to refuse her. *But you'd have to live in.*

Yvonne's chest lurches. Nursing. Study. An image flashes up of a blue cap perched on her head, perhaps even the starched veil of the nursing sister. Then: *I can't*, she says. *There's Sharon.*

We could find somewhere for her. A children's home. Do Matron's sharp vowels soften a little? *It would only be temporary.*

The words 'children's home' shock an answer from her. *No.* It is immediate, as if it has been waiting in her body for this. *No, Matron. I won't do that.*

Matron blinks. That is all that betrays her. She says, *Think about it, Yvonne,* and drops her eyes once more to the sheaf of papers – they bear the letterhead of the Mater Hospital – and the conversation is over. She is dismissed.

Back on the ward, her heart is still clattering around in her chest. It isn't the impact of saying *No* – though she will feel this later, on the bus home – nor the generosity of the offer, which moves her, catches her breath. It isn't Matron's deft disguise of her own surprise and disappointment. It is that this woman she admires more than any other, a woman she looks to for approval, would assume she would trade a future for a child.

He is three years old. Flashes of memory – thin, insubstantial – begin here. Fleeting images and sensations of warmth, tenderness even, from his aunt, Adriana. Stepping in and out of the empty shape where a mother should be. The shape where a father should be too, because Michael is emotionally as well as physically absent from him now, unwilling or unable to express his feelings for this son he has been separated from for many months. For this son whose body is now shockingly distorted, no longer the baby boy he remembers, the boy born in his own image and of his own hopes.

Unlike other parents of children in rehabilitation, Michael visits his son rarely and does not take him home, not for a weekend, not for a day. Peter has no sense of family now beyond the nursing staff around him, has no sense of home. Nothing is regular, nothing is predictable. So over the next eighteen months of distressing physiotherapy and manipulation, the confinement in rigid steel contraptions to prevent further distortion of his spine and limbs, there is only and occasionally Adriana, her kind face bent to him in encouragement, her voice softer than the nurses and therapists around him and more trustworthy.

But not enough. The paralysis that has robbed him of movement has gripped his emotions too. A coldness has settled around his heart; by the time he turns four he has lost his optimism, his child's trust in others and any sense of the world as benign. He has already begun the process of toughening up, of total self-reliance, of growing a thick skin that is impervious to pain in all its guises. Deep within him, he already knows he'll need this skin to survive.

At the Far West Home, Peter's wasted left leg is fitted with a calliper. For the first time in more than a year he is allowed – made to – stand upright again, and pain of a completely different texture replaces the old. His legs have forgotten how to move his body around, how to swing his feet, one in front of the other. He stands and cries and falls and cries and is made to pick himself up. The procedure is repeated until he absolutely understands that no one will help him. He will have to help himself.

With this knowledge irreversibly planted in his brain, he learns haltingly, grudgingly, to walk with the hated calliper. When he falls – and he falls frequently – he doesn't cry now though the pain is intense and the indignity worse, and he refuses to raise his eyes. Only Adriana, who occasionally takes him out for a day, ever sees a glimmer of hurt, of frustration, when he stumbles. It might last seconds, no more, but it is enough for her or anyone to see the depth of suffering behind the almond eyes, beyond the shrivelled limb.

His stay at the Far West seems endless, but he is eventually moved to Belmont, an after-care facility near Newcastle, where he learns, some time in 1953, that his father has bought a shop in Dungog and has asked if Peter can join him there. He is confused and unsure what it means when the matron tells him the news: *Your father is coming*, she says in the tone of someone who has found a precious gem, *You're going home.*

When she isn't on night shift at Clinton or the café, she and Sharon sit at the top of the back stairs at Cannon Hill after dinner and read or sing. Sometimes it's a song Sharon knows the words to: 'How Much is That Doggy in the Window?' or 'Bimbo'. But the little girl loves it just as much when her mother sings her own favourites. Sharon knows they make her mother happy. It might be 'Play To Me Gypsy', or 'The Donkey Serenade' but best of all is 'The Lion Sleeps Tonight'. *A wimoweh, a wimoweh.* As her mother's soft voice floats out over the darkened backyard, Sharon stares at the shifting shapes of clothes line and shrubs and vegetable garden, thunderbox, woodpile, choko vine furring the crooked teeth of the paling fence, and imagines it all jungle, black but for the glow of a sleeping lion's mane.

For one of Yvonne's nights off, Mary Sessarago surprises her with a ticket to the opera. *Rigoletto* at the Theatre Royal. She has seen the pause in Yvonne whenever a resident is playing

Verdi or Chopin, the twist of her body towards the music – and perhaps she sees some latent quality, some unmet potential that might be fostered, enriched, cultivated. They catch a taxi into Queen Street, and, when the curtain goes up, Yvonne sits watching, listening, trying not to betray too much, as big, beautiful voices bound and reach around ornate plaster ceilings and lamp-lit walls. But beneath her best dress her heart leaps to match the voices, to match the rapture, the enchantment she hasn't allowed herself to feel for years.

The seeds of this enchantment might have begun at her father's side, listening to the wireless, to broadcasts of *The Merry Widow* or *William Tell*. Her beloved, contrary father, who values the classics in word and music and oils, who loves the scholarly but robbed his children of school. Let's give him the benefit of the doubt, and say that here, beckoning his daughter to the chair beside him, encouraging her to listen, to untangle the exotic sounds, he tries to make up for that. The beauty of language, the weight of history in the stories, the moral tales. She sits beside him and opens her heart.

People say that the love of opera is immediate and rapid, even physical, like love at first sight. Perhaps this is what happened to my teenaged mother, a collision of senses: her father breathing beside her, the music soaring, becoming visual, seeping beneath her vulnerable, adolescent skin.

Opera, the ads say now, *life amplified*. Though from this perspective I wonder how, to my twenty-two year old mother, anything of Rossini's or Verdi's or Puccini's could possibly be bigger than her own life and the tragedy that engulfed it. Or perhaps that's the point: perhaps the passion and drama of opera reflected her own life back to her in a way she could cope with. Perhaps it glamorises its tragedy. There, on the stage or just the wireless, are her own emotions, all their extremities, expressed in a way she is not permitted to express them. Perhaps opera gives her grief full voice, gives her a way to grieve, a way to give the events of her life a shape. In these stories she could see that this, this loneliness and heartbreak, isn't the end of the story. It may not even be the middle.

They stand behind a picket fence, wearing look-alike floral dresses that hug their curves. Yvonne and Shirley are twenty-two or twenty-three, and the dresses suggest a festive occasion, summer, light hearts. And that is just how Shirley looks: she's smiling a wide, joyous smile, her head thrown back, her body angled playfully. She's having a ball, flirting with the camera, and probably with the photographer. But beside her my mother is serious, almost grim, staring the photographer down. She might be saying, *Don't you dare.*

There is a quip about this photo, famous in my family, and we all know it by heart. *It looks like Yvonne lost a sixpence,* we'd chorus when it appeared in the album, *and Shirley found it.* My mother would laugh along with the rest of us and then disappear to fold the washing. These days, when I look at the photo and remember the joke, I can't raise a smile. I can see the joke for what it is: an attempt to represent Yvonne's sadness as something else, something palatable like jealousy, or sourness at losing a bright coin. It isn't callous; rather a re-working of her grief into something bearable for everyone. We had to:

leaving that picture open to interpretation was too dangerous, too freighted with loss. With the echo of a misery that stalked all our lives.

My mother didn't like the photo. Perhaps it was a reminder, and preserved that time and the person she was forever. Contrary to the promise of happy family photos – you will *always* be happy – she didn't want to always be the way she was there. She didn't want that person, that woman, commemorated. She was in the process of becoming a different one.

And so she gradually begins to reclaim her life: occasionally relenting, she goes out with one of her admirers, or in a group. A milkshake at the Pig'n'Whistle in town, a local football game where she sits placidly while the men grow passionate and even Val shouts, *Hit 'em in the bread-basket!* Later, as friends dissect the game and Val regrets a missed try, Yvonne shakes her head. *More brawn than brains*, she says with a sigh.

She quickly learns to expect disappointment. Each suitor falls short; they seem hollow, as if nothing ties them, grounds them. They have no interest in her daughter, and lose interest in Yvonne too once Sharon is mentioned. There is one in particular, he's in the football team. He'd courted her in the days before she met Michael, and now that she is single once more, he sidles back into her life. Like Michael he is dark and good-looking, with Valentino eyes and thick black hair swept back from his face.

Yvonne is flattered by his attention; perhaps it returns her to a simpler world before Michael, before disaster. She even takes Sharon along to a game. But it soon becomes clear his plans do not include her child. He is always polite and pleasant around Sharon, but one day, sitting with Yvonne in her parents' kitchen, he glances at the little girl and hisses: She should have been *ours*. She'd turned her face to him and understood at once. Should have been ours, he'd said. Not *might* be ours.

That's all it takes. In one brief sentence Yvonne sees the line he has drawn, that it will always be there. She wants much more. She wants something where no lines exist, in which her daughter's presence is non-negotiable. She won't see the footballer again, doesn't lift her eyes to anyone, stops looking.

She is sitting on the steps of a flat in Kent Street — a working-class street following a ridge that drops to New Farm on one side and The Valley on the other — waiting for her friend Olga to come home. Olga is a workmate, and Yvonne has walked fifteen minutes from Clinton to deliver a message about a shift. It is a hot day sometime early in 1954 — we don't know which month, we know only about the weather — and she is happy to sit there on the shady side of the old house which has been, like many of the others around it, turned over to cheap flats with coin-operated hot water and toilets down the back.

The sudden trill of a telephone might have broken her reverie, but if it didn't perhaps it is this: the lithe body of a man, shirtless, materialising beside her as he hurries up the steps and into another flat to answer the phone. There isn't time to notice anything else except a tan, and horn-rimmed glasses, and an overly serious expression. Still, he is polite when he edges past her on his way back, asking if she is waiting for someone, telling her that he lives in the flat next to Olga's and saw her go out. She might have noticed, then, the jutting cheekbones, the lilting accent, but he disappears again quickly towards a makeshift shed in the backyard. Later, when he passes her again and shrugs and from politeness offers her some coffee, she declines, and soon afterwards gives up on Olga and walks away.

Years afterwards, she will tell him she was first attracted by his nonchalance, by the sting she feels at being barely noticed. She was, she will say, not used to being ignored.

It is some weeks later, a rare Saturday afternoon off. Yvonne and Shirley are lounging on Olga's ancient couch, their legs tucked beneath them. Yvonne watches Shirley file her nails. *What's his name?* Shirley says suddenly, without raising her head from her task. *Your neighbour, the one with the accent?*

Olga is brewing tea in the kitchenette; she looks at her friends over a bottle of milk. *There's a couple with accents*, she says, pouring milk into a jug.

The cute one. Shirley peers at her finished nails and lifts her eyes. *Not the Russian, Olga. The one in the workshop.*

Yvonne grins. *It's Arne*, she says. *He's a Swede.* And seeing Shirley's brows shoot upwards: *Olga told me.*

Shirley unfurls her legs and stands. *Well*, she says languidly, *I wonder if the Swede would like a cup of tea.* She stirs sugar into one of the cups Olga has poured and disappears down the stairs.

A couple of hours later, after Shirley has made one more trip to the shed to retrieve Arne's cup and reluctantly left for night shift, and after they've played Olga's records one more time, Yvonne looks at her watch and grimaces. *Missed my tram*, she says, glancing about for her handbag. *Mum will kill me.* She hurries outside just as Arne locks the door of his shed and turns towards the stairs.

She hears Olga's voice behind her: *Yvonne's missed her tram!*

Yvonne's face blazes crimson. She frowns, keeps walking, but in a beat he says, *Would you like a lift?*

She hesitates and glares at Olga, who smiles, innocent. Flicks a glance at Arne. Then: *All right*, she says, hugging her bag to her chest. And then, *thank you.*

This is what she will remember: in the time it took to drive from New Farm to Cannon Hill, certain things were said and certain things revealed. Nothing about loss or heartbreak, not then. Things that mattered nonetheless: nuances of temperament, of personal qualities – loyalty, honour, responsibility – and traces of the hope they both carried with them like a secret. She didn't know that at the time, not consciously. But later, looking back, she could follow the breadcrumb trail of their hearts: various words, phrases, looks, the rise and fall of a voice, the answers given to questions so casual they couldn't guess their lives depended on them.

Their first date is a movie. He arrives to collect her at Clinton bearing chocolates – Cadbury *Roses* – and still wearing his work clothes: long khaki trousers and shirt, chest pocket bulging with small screwdrivers, pencils, and his sleeves rolled up. The uniform of his working life. He is late. She purses her lips at this, and at the brown monochrome of his wardrobe.

But there is no rush of impatience or anger. The plain clothes are a kind of relief. He is no peacock, no Michael; she has no need to look beyond his clothes to what they mean and what they might hide. She is intrigued by the strengths in him they might suggest. Still, she is carefully dressed herself – a dress with a fitted waist, her wavy hair brushed back – and all this takes her by surprise just a little, his clothes, her own response. She smiles at him there on the cool verandah of Clinton as he proffers the chocolates and apologises in that engaging accent for being late. She keeps smiling, an ironic, crooked smile, as he glances down at his khakis and shrugs and tells her he meant to change, and says with the shy grin of a boy, *I forgot the time.*

And so it goes. One date, then another. It doesn't take her long to convince herself. He picks her up in the utility that carries all his working paraphernalia, brushing the passenger seat first with his open palm. Riding next to him, she feels something like safety, like the ground has finally formed beneath her feet. It is like a kindness. She feels it, reads it in the air between them, this gentleness telegraphed back and forth. Well, she thinks, yes; a kind man. It is possible.

She asks him about his work, his country. He tells her about circuits and currents and conduction, that he has loved electric motors all his life. Batteries and sparks and detonations. She laughs at his stories of childhood, the neighbour's mailboxes destroyed with thumbs of nitro-glycerine, the cigarettes that fizz and explode in his father's fingers. The numbing cold. He is, he tells her, seeking the sun. Warmth. But he doesn't know, he says with a careful smile, if he'll stay.

When he asks her about her own day's work she brushes her skirt over her knees with her palms, once, twice, as if she is soothing a nervous child. She recounts stories of Matron and her patients, but his last sentence has unnerved her. He may not stay. In the days that follow she thinks of him constantly, his decency, his unvanquished optimism, the compelling mix of adult confidence with the gentleness of a child. Something, she realises, has shifted in her: she has begun to trust him. This is confirmed on the day she asks him about the boy in the photograph on his kitchen wall.

This is what he tells her: his son's name is Lennart. Bertil Lennart for his uncle, the names interchangeable in the Swedish way. In the picture he is perhaps four years old, with blond hair cut in the Prince Valiant style that lingers from his father's own childhood. The photographer has done a good job, she thinks: the little boy smiles easily at something away from the camera, his eyes shine. She looks from the photo to the man and back again. It's hard to see in his still-forming face, but he might have his father's chin, perhaps his nose.

He tells her he was married early, hastily, one Swedish midsummer when he was just twenty-one. *Too young*, he says with a shrug. This movement of face and shoulders is meant to say the un-sayable, and she sees this and doesn't ask for more. But he does tell her of his shock to learn, after he had fled to sea, that he had won custody of Lennart. For now, he says, Lennart is happy with his uncle and aunt. When he has a new home and is properly settled, he hopes Lennart will come.

Yvonne stands before the photo, her head tilted, and understands more than she hears. What is missing from Arne's story is hidden like a prayer between his words, in the way they are spoken. There is a quiet dignity in his voice, in the neat, careful way he sets out cups for coffee in the little flat, slices cake. Watching and listening, she feels the first stirrings of a love that might be for him and might be for herself. The self she hasn't yet forgiven.

She turns and looks at him. And her own words, when she says them, might have been formed long before and lay waiting: *Would you like to meet my daughter?*

A week later they are standing, Yvonne and Sharon, in freshly ironed dresses and clean shoes, on the end of Bomberry Street in Cannon Hill. She has told him she doesn't want to be picked up at home. She isn't ready for her parents' scrutiny yet, their opinions; she doesn't want to subject this new and lovely notion – her fledgling trust – to anyone's critical eye. Besides, it is her life; her choices are her own. She has earned them, her right to them, in the hardest possible way.

Here he is, finally. Late, as usual. He walks around to the passenger side, bends formally to shake Sharon's hand, and they climb into the ute, onto the newly scrubbed bench seat. Sharon sits back with her hands at her sides and her legs stick out in mid-air. Yvonne has made sure her socks are neatly turned down, her shoes spotless.

They stop in Brunswick Street and buy cakes at McDonald's Cake Shop, then follow the tram tracks to Kent Street. In the tiny flat Arne makes coffee, pours orange cordial. She watches him move around, stopping occasionally to bend towards Sharon, to ask her about her playmates, remark on her pretty shoes. She hears the soft inflection in his voice. He's tentative, she can see, finding his way. The three of them sit at the kitchen table and talk.

But after an hour, Sharon begins to fade. Yvonne sees her body slump a little, her eyes growing heavy. Then realises Arne has noticed too – without a pause in the conversation he extends his arms, and wordlessly, Sharon slips from her chair, climbs into his lap and falls asleep. Arne looks over at her with a smile, Yvonne thinks, as wide as Texas. *Just like a little troll!* he beams. Yvonne tries to imagine the trolls of her primary school readers, and can't. It doesn't matter. In this dim kitchen that smells of coffee and machine oil she is seeing something else, something fundamental: that with this man her child might be cherished. She looks at them opposite her, the easy arrangement of limbs, how relaxed he is, how entirely happy. They keep talking softly while Sharon sleeps. She knows they've reached some kind of marker in this relationship, something informed by a child's trust.

There would, of course, be a proper proposal and acceptance, later, and a ring, but this was the day she suspended her disbelief. People might behave well, after all, a happy ending might be possible. A decent life, even joy, might be salvageable, after all. He's told her about salvage; has seen ships crippled in the ocean's maw, and the re-making of something out of loss. This day, she'll think later, is the day she begins to believe again. In the idea of happiness, in a future. That they might be, for each other, a path towards forgiveness, towards hope.

When Mary Sessarago is told of the engagement, she looks at Yvonne and nods, wary. She has seen and met the Swedish engineer, but he's a newcomer, hard to gauge. She says, *He's no oil painting is he, Yvonne?* – and Yvonne feels she has been slapped. It is true he is no movie star, no Valentino. But how to explain how lovely she finds him? She searches for ways and gives up. Instead, she says – indignant, steely – *No, Matron.* A pause. *And Mr Sessarago is no Mr Universe.* As she strides away she can hear the soft eruption of Matron's laughter.

Sharon doesn't remember the first time she met our father. Only picnics in grassy fields, a blanket spread. The three of them and her own belonging there, inside that tight circle. There are sandwiches or, thrillingly, a fire with sausages speared and cooked on a stick. *This is how we did it when I was small,* he tells her as they search beneath trees for just the right stick. She watches as he sharpens its end with a pen-knife. What she'd give for a go at that.

There are games and talk and a sensation of comfort in his presence, theirs. Because at these times our mother is different. She smiles more. Even when Arne – the *Kjell* has been swiftly dropped – brings out his camera. Yvonne hates cameras. At first she squeezes her lips together but then she gives in, lets Sharon wriggle in close. Even at four Sharon can feel the softening in her mother then; can feel her limbs relax when they lean together, the brush of her cheek against her own. The little girl looks straight at the Box Brownie and smiles. She loves it when Arne takes her picture. He takes a long minute with its levers and buttons before he says, *Say sheese.* And she loves the way he talks, the funny sounds, especially the sound of her name when he says it. *Charon*. She leans into her mother, breathes in her musky skin, smiles a toothy smile and says *sheese*.

One day – a drive in the country, another picnic – the camera comes out again and they wait for the click, for the smile that means he got it. But then Yvonne pulls away and goes to Arne. Reaches for the camera. *Now one of you two*, she says, and Arne grins and swaps places. His hand light on Sharon's arm.

And here are the photographs, more than fifty years later, pressed precisely into the family album. Here are Yvonne and Sharon, Arne and Sharon, Sharon perched on the glossy hood of a car clutching the stick and the cooked sausage. Here, in black and white, is how determined they are. It's the three of them, and it's not enough to say it, so they photograph it. Making it their story, making it tangible, something other people can see.

Now, when we look at these photographs together, my sister and I, this is what Sharon sees: a child with her mother, a child with her father. As simple, and as complex, as that.

Peter's first real memories are of absence. And of difference. At six, he is old enough to know he is different on several counts. His right leg, primarily. He wears a calliper and a built-up shoe, and even though he's taught himself to run, after a fashion, it isn't like other boys. It is the lop-sided lunge of a wounded animal, desperate to survive. And there is this other thing about these boys he knows: they have mothers. Female creatures who look after them. At home he asks about his own. Does he have one? Where is she? His father's answer is simple, blunt: she is a nothing, a prostitute, Michael tells him. She ran off. Ran away from him, and with a German. The detail of this confounds him — a *German* — but whatever its intended effect, it doesn't work on Peter. If he has a mother, he will find her.

This urge becomes stronger when his father inexplicably disappears one day and doesn't return, not for a long time. They are in Dungog now, another town, another shop. Peter is sent to stay with an elderly Greek couple while Michael is away, but his confusion is deepened by the answers they give to his questions: *He's just gone away for a bit, he'll be back soon.* None of this is helped by the kids at school, who smirk at his callipers and call him a 'crip'. He hates the callipers. He hates putting them on in the mornings and the painful and slow walk to school; the way they seem to cage his whole body. He steals glances at the strong, perfect limbs of other boys and wonders what it feels like to really run.

He misses his father. Before he left, Michael had made new efforts with him, doing things other fathers did. He's bought him a piano accordion – *A Greek boy should learn Greek music*, Michael says when he brings it home. And begins to take Peter about with him, to the markets, or visiting. A friend has a farm outside town; sometimes they will take the rifle and go rabbiting. Peter loves this, not the shooting so much as the new proximity to his father. It is a fledgling sense of mateship he feels nowhere else. But now, without a word of explanation, Michael has disappeared.

Flakes of week-old confetti lie in drifts against the sandstone buttresses of St Paul's Presbyterian Church in Spring Hill. But inside the air is new, splendid. Love, optimism and courage are being celebrated, all the virtues that have brought them here: patience, forbearance, hope. And a certain amount of luck.

She takes her vows the way she's always wanted to, with a sense of holiness and witness. She wants this marriage to be visible – they both do – they want the solidity of the stone walls and the insistent beauty of the organ music to firmly stamp this as the beginning. To firmly obliterate the past. The wonderfully named Reverend Pashen blesses them in a voice that booms to the high rafters and the clerestory, and she feels as she has always felt here at services on Christmas Eve and infrequent Sundays: as if her whole body has been washed in clear, cool water. As if she is new.

This is what others see, her parents, brothers and sisters, their handful of friends: her dress of blue lace, ballerina length, a spray of flowers and netting that takes the place of a veil, that catches the rice and fresh confetti they're showered with as they leave the church. Daisies and orange blossom and a horseshoe for luck. The colour of her dress and the absence of a veil are her only concessions to the past.

But mostly, they see this: the softness in her face and his. And especially they notice his hands, the way they hesitate just a little before they settle on her back, on her arms, and these small things tell them she is cherished. Really, this is all they want for her, all those who have seen her face look different, clenched shut with pain. Now they see what is there in the glances she exchanges with this man, the possibility of a good and happy life, and they can forgive him even his foreignness, even the voice that curls into sounds they often find hard to follow.

At the reception rooms at Coolden, around the corner from Clinton, there are speeches, telegrams from Sweden and from ships in various ports, a cake with a blue plastic bride and groom and, of course, bluebirds. And everyone looks now for the ordinary moments between them, the unguarded, the un-photographed. The way she tips her head towards his when he speaks; his shy, shuffling attempts at the bridal waltz, his self-conscious smile as she leads him. His hands gripping hers. The guests all clap at the end of the dance, and when they raise their glasses it isn't to faultless waltzing but to gentleness, two people fitting their steps around each other, finding a new way.

It is a cold day in early winter, 1955, and today is the day he has resolved to do it. His father is gone, and he needs to find his mother. School seems an intolerable prospect, the callipers, the jeers. Suddenly, this morning, he feels for the first time the weightlessness of giving up. There is no one or nothing here he cares about; nothing he feels constrained by. There is just the small matter of money.

He leaves the house, waving to the old couple as if he is going to school, but heads instead to home, to the shop, where a friend of Michael's is temporarily in charge. His chance comes when the man hurries out for more tomatoes, leaving the till unattended. It takes only seconds to snatch ten shillings and be gone. If the air around the till or the front counter is somehow disturbed, if there is still faint movement in the coloured plastic strips that curtain the front doorway, there is no one to see. Peter is gone, his absence unnoticed.

The small crippled boy is no stranger at the station at Dungog, not to the station master nor to the townspeople who mill around the platform, waiting for the Sydney train. He turns up here on his frequent wanders around town, dragging his shortened leg but always smiling. Watching people, the snorting engines, the movement of cases and freight. So no one is surprised by his presence here today, and when the train comes everyone is far too preoccupied with getting on and finding a seat to notice the boy hoist himself up the steps of the last carriage and disappear into one of its compartments. On the two-hour journey, everyone on board assumes a small boy who is lame in one leg will be with his parents, so no one is alarmed to see him staggering up and down.

At Central Station he tumbles from the train but remains upright, somehow, and is immediately swallowed up by the crowd. He careers between lines and groups of people, bumping against handbags and Gladstone bags, arching his neck to see the curved roof, the glass, the iron lacework. People move in fast-flowing currents around him. He pauses occasionally to look up at the female faces beneath hats, at dresses both puffy and straight. Handbags looped over arms. But it's all a blur of hurry and scurry and heels clicking as though they're alive; people who know who they are and where they're going. He tries not to feel overwhelmed.

And then he does what he has come here to do. He chooses arbitrary faces, limps towards them, tugs at their sleeves. *Hey*, he says, looking up at each one keenly, *do you know my mother? Do you know where she is?*

Sometimes they don't even hear him or see him and sometimes they look at him sadly and say, *Oh, are you lost?* If they do he shakes his head and ducks away, as quickly as he can in a crowd. He has made it all this way and he isn't going to be thwarted easily, so when he sees an alarmed expression on a kind face he tries to hide behind pillars and doors. But he is such a clear target, and it doesn't take long before a man and a woman in police uniforms swoop. They are kind to him; he likes kindness and he likes them. They take him to an office in the train station, ask him where he lives, how he got here. Give him biscuits and cordial.

Back at home with the old people, who don't thrash him as he knows his father would but send him to bed without his dinner, he lies awake and he isn't unhappy. His stomach rumbles and hurts a bit, but he purses his lips and remembers his day, what it delivered. Not his mother, not this time, but something else: the delicious sensation of escape. Of being alone, away from this place and all the wounding eyes and hands. It is a feeling he will seek and find again and again, as he runs towards some confused idea of freedom, some notion of a mother. There's no danger in it, none that he can see; he isn't scared of being alone, not even at seven. From then on he's only scared of one thing: being caught.

A wedding, a honeymoon. Dream and reality. Who could blame her if, in these first days when happiness hovers, close as her husband's breath, she imagines, sometimes – perhaps hallucinates – the shape of her son in a crowd?

They begin their honeymoon trip on the suitably named Darling Downs. It is winter, and in Stanthorpe he holds her all through the chill night, waiting for her body to relax against his. He can wait a lifetime if he has to.

They wake to a new life together, and a landscape made delicate by frost and ice. The water in the car's radiator and hoses is frozen. He shudders, feeling the glance of thirty-one deep winters in his bones.

She has never been to Sydney. But thinks it an interesting idea when he suggests it. He says they can see the bridge, the harbour, the shops, and he can go down to the docks to meet the *Citos*, one of the ships he serves as chandler. She has no idea they are journeying so close to Peter. He might be anywhere, though she assumes Cairns, somewhere in the north. There is nothing in the sound of the word *Sydney* that suggests him, any more than a thousand other words do, every hour, every day.

She pushes these words and images away as soon as they appear. This is what she tells herself: he will have a new family. He will speak a language she doesn't understand. There will be a woman he calls 'mother' watching him run about in splendid sunshine. He will not remember the eyes that saw him first, the smell of her, the way his body fitted into hers when she held him. This is knowledge she can barely concede; when it enters her head she defeats it by almost wishing it is true. If he has forgotten her he will not feel the pain she still feels every day.

She couldn't guess what he looks like now – though sometimes, watching Sharon sleep, she imagines she can see him there, the heart-shaped face and dark lashes. Of course, she has no inkling of the paralysed leg, that he wears pain in his face.

This is how it goes: they are standing on the street outside Central Station waiting for a cab. She's tired but she's happy. They've already walked around the Gardens and Circular Quay, the wind flicking at their coats, their hair; stopped for tea near the Rocks. The town is grubby, she thinks, and too big, but she is in love with sandstone, its historical intimations. History: at these moments she misses her schooling as if it were a friend.

From the Rocks they've gazed over at the bridge, its poetic span. Now as they wait she steps idly inside the station, peers at the arched steel of its ceiling, thinking: it mirrors the bridge. A train heaves up to a platform, people spill out, filling the space with colour and movement.

And she sees, out of the corner of her eye, a small, dark-haired boy limping towards the entrance. She watches as he pulls on the arm of a passing woman, his eyes turned up to her, before he lurches on. Something lurches in her too, something gives, her blood quickens. His face. The possibility. It is beyond all odds, yet in her head and heart she has imagined just such a scene – how many times? – the accidental glance, the momentary glimpse. She raises her hand then, opens her mouth to say his name, it seems it's been waiting there on her lips – *Peter* – since the day he disappeared. But then he is swallowed up by the tide of people on the platform, and, though she pulls her arm from her husband's, her hurried steps instinctive, following – he is gone.

After the wedding and the honeymoon there is, briefly, a tiny flat in Kent Street, just down the road from his old one, with a kitchen and bedroom and hot water for coins. She keeps working at Clinton; they save every penny not needed for food and rent and hot baths. He has his eye on a property across the road: a shopfront with a house and flats attached. There's a big yard with trees, a garage, a workshop, a chicken coop. It's solid ground, it's everything he wants. Perfect. He begins a long process of bargaining with the Scottish man who owns it – and within months they're renting the shop and the smallest of the flats with a view to purchase.

Here too there are only three rooms, and it's a squeeze. Sharon sleeps on a narrow bed just inside the front door, there is a kitchen lit by sun through tall louvres, a bathroom, a bedroom. They dig in, pull the purse-strings even tighter. A pound of mince makes enough rissoles for three meals, or is stirred with vegetables and Worcestershire sauce and served on toast. Three times. No more new clothes; shoes wear out and are mended. She digs the last of the lipstick from the tube with her little finger. Gets Val to cut her hair.

At Clinton, Arne is called upon when fuses blow and lights go out or the wiring needs renewing. He will often sit while his wife finishes in the kitchen, flicking through a newspaper and sipping tea, or watching Sharon and Paul, Matron's son, playing out the back. Yvonne smiles wryly as Matron stops to chat with him: he has completely won her over.

He is at Clinton one early evening when the cry goes up: the Mad Hatter is gone again. In her thin nightie, her hats all awry, she has run for it, up Bowen Terrace and God knows where. He and Yvonne give chase, and he is faster, glimpsing the Hatter as she nears Brunswick Street. She flees – nimble for a woman her age, her nightie long and loose and no impediment – towards the squat stone mansion that is Lambourne, home to the Catholic Archbishop. He watches her disappear, wraith-like, through the high iron gates and into its darkened grounds.

Where he finds her soon enough; she is out of breath now, slumped near a soaring silky oak, triumphant. But hatless. It doesn't take much to convince her to come back with him. He takes her by the arm as he would his wife, or mother, and slowly they proceed back to Clinton, the Hatter throwing back her head, every now and then, and laughing to the sky.

The disaster of the first wife had taught Michael a lesson: the next bride had to be Greek. A good Greek girl who understood her place in a marriage. Who knew what was expected: cooking, cleaning, hard work and no questions. He needed all that. But more than anything he needed two things: a woman who would accept and care for another woman's son, and a woman who would not run away.

So, you have a new mother, Panayotis, Michael says as if he has pulled her from a hat. *Say hello.* The woman steps forward and speaks in the same fast Greek as his father. Her name is Sophia. *Sof-ee-ya.* A nice enough name, Peter thinks. It's the only thing he *can* think; his head is noisy with the surprise of his father in the doorway, home at last, and then this magic trick of a *new mother.* Peter blinks. The helpless joy at seeing his father again is swallowed up, gulped down, at the sight of the woman.

Peter looks at her carefully from beneath his lashes. *Kalimera,* he says quietly. *Good morning.* And to his father, in English, *where did she come from?*

Something blazes in Michael's eyes and then subsides. *From Greece,* he says with a flourish of a laugh, his arm round Sophia's waist. *And seeing you're so smart it's your job to teach her English.*

So that is how it goes. In the Sunshine Café in Dungog, the small, wavy-haired woman goes about her new chores with the boy, cooking, cleaning, loading drinks. As they bend and reach and shuffle behind the counter, Peter seizes on everyday things and touches them or lifts them towards her. *Phonos,* he will say, holding the black receiver, *telephone.* Slowly, carefully. Taking an order, *Thank you* – he looks at her, nodding – *efharisto.* She repeats the words, watching his mouth, her lips clumsy around the strange sounds. *Tank. You.* In this way the two feel each other out, they gauge each other through sound, the weight of a word or a syllable, a smile or a frown or a sigh of impatience.

Her skin shines with sweat as she works. It gives her a particular smell, or so he thinks when they're working together, not good not bad, the kind of sour sweetness of fruit left too long in a hot schoolbag. Watching her – her uncertain eyes that ignore him much of the time because they are following Michael, the hands that can scrub and clean, all right, but never touch him – he wonders if this is what mothers are like, what mothers do. He slips into sleep at night imagining his real mother's skin. His real mother's smell.

She isn't his real mother but she has a mother's shape. A kind of Adriana shape, a bit baggy at the edges, like the mothers he sees walking other children to school. His father's edges are softer too since he's been back; he's not shouting. Not as much. Still, everyone who comes into the café knows who's boss, Peter can see that. They listen to him in a particular way, they pay attention. Sophia does too.

For a couple of weeks there is a lot of this kind of talking and listening between the Greek men who come to the café, and then suddenly – it seems sudden to Peter, he hasn't seen it coming – they are moving again. Maitland. It is, he thinks, his fourth move in six years, not counting the hospitals and convalescent homes. He goes through them on his fingers: Sydney-Junee-Dungog-Maitland, his hands making the map of Michael's steady track back towards the city. The sure circle of his own path in the direction of that other mother, the one he feels he might already know.

Michael gets the new café for a song. The lower part of the two-storey building has been through Maitland's recent flood. He repairs and reassembles it by hand. It is the classic Greek café: all polished wood and mirrored booths and milkshake machines lined up on the bench. Sweets in glass jars, cups and saucers, the silver cash register that pings when its money drawer snaps shut.

It is beautiful, Peter can see that, but he knows what the shiny surfaces and well-stacked shelves stand for: work. The routine in the new place is the same as before, and it's hard. Up early for breakfast, load and organise the drinks fridge, Coke, Fanta, 7-Up, milk, then walk to school. Home for lunch, help with the rush hour – he stands on a banana box and helps to make milkshakes – and the same again after school. Sometimes he works in the shop until after nine at night. On weekends there's Greek school. More shop work.

But despite the work, he feels settled; he might even be happy. Except. He goes to school and does his chores and thinks of new words to teach Sophia, and still there is a part of him that doesn't trust the calm, the peace. A part that isn't surprised when things begin to change. He kicks himself for his lapse: he'd let his guard down, got complacent, allowed a glimmer of hope and optimism to seed in his tough little heart.

It all begins with something straightforward enough: Sophia is pregnant. Michael grins widely when he says this. His hands and words grow gentle around Sophia and even around the boy. Peter might be pleased too, if he could understand what it means, for him, for his ordinary life. A baby, he ponders. Well. A little brother or sister might be good, he supposes. Everyone around them seems to think so.

But though he can never be sure how or why, his whole world shrinks and sours about this time. The only thing that delineates the calm period from the chaotic is Sophia's accident. She is crossing the street, heavy-bellied, and miscalculates. A car clips her body and she falls. It is her equilibrium that is most bruised; it is her confidence, as much as her skin or bones, that feels the shock and slumps onto the cold bitumen. A doctor confirms it: she is fine, the baby is fine. But Peter knows otherwise. It's in her eyes when she chips him if he's too slow with his chores, when she heaves her swollen body up to the counter, elbows him aside, ignoring his chirped words of English.

Small children are always displaced by the arrival of a new sibling, no matter the age difference, their happiness or otherwise, or whether or not they're aware of their own anger. It's natural. Here in the house is a new version of themselves filling a hole they didn't even know was there, a space that has opened up like a trapdoor. They have to shuffle aside to allow for it, or be pushed. The landscape of the family, their mother's face, will never look the same.

When Sophia finally delivers her baby, Peter feels something break. It's a boy. In a culture that circles around the role and power of first-born sons, Peter knows, even at eight, who this baby is. What he is: the *real* first-born son. Not the child of an Australian *putana*, a street girl, a runaway. Newborn George is the child of a decent Greek woman, and perfect in every way. Ten fingers, ten toes, and two good legs. Peter looks at his little brother and sees that they are not the same.

Whatever harmony has existed is short-lived. Michael's gambling is like a rash that lives just below the skin, benign for days. Sometimes he can just ignore it, before the itch builds and the urge to scratch is unbearable, irresistible. The more and harder he scratches the more and harder he needs to. It's a savage pleasure that turns him raw and angry. Within months he begins again to disappear, a whole day, several. He starts at the markets in Sydney and moves on to the Athenaeum Club where the poker goes all night. The air at home stretches thin and brittle.

When it finally cracks open Peter feels the percussion in his body, though it is Sophia's that is marked: a red welt in the shape of Michael's hand. He has been away again, Newcastle or Sydney, who knows, but this time it's been three days. Longer than before. And Sophia left at home with Peter, the shop, the new baby. A few words of broken English and her exhaustion growing.

When Michael brushes past him in the hallway, Peter can see what Sophia can't: the danger in the set of his mouth. She opens hers to complain, and he hits her. Through the wall Peter hears a sheet snapping in the wind, a door smacking shut. Sophia cries out. She is taken by surprise, Peter can tell, and she keeps yelling, and Michael hits her again. Then she is quiet.

Peter, a little boy in callipers who is no stranger to the sting of his father's hand, feels a shock in the part of himself he has learned to keep secret. In that soft, vulnerable place he feels a kind of nausea; he has never, he thinks, seen his father strike anyone else before. It happens again and again – she answers back, she is too slow, she can't keep the baby quiet – and the nausea burrows in. He wants it to stop, he wants to get away from it. That word, *away*, becomes a talisman, it goes around and around in his head when he lies in bed at night or as he swings his caged leg up the street after school. Until the day he finds himself at a train station again.

He doesn't know it's the beginning of something. Can't see the shape of the next decade forming on the road in front of him. He knows only that he can't bear it, the sound of flesh hitting flesh. There's the road, the train tracks, both leading away from that sound, and he doesn't think any further than that. Sometimes he gets to the next town, sometimes he's picked up at Maitland station. But always the police find him and return him to his father. He is chastised and belted. The cycle begins again.

It is broken occasionally, startlingly, when Michael pulls him from his bed on dark mornings and tells him to dress, they are going to the market. Just the two of them. It takes Peter by surprise each time; he might mistake the gesture for kindness. Rather than a police instruction to *keep the boy at home*. But Peter knows by now what to say and what not to say, when to keep his own counsel. So he quietly enjoys his father's proximity, the bluster and noise of the markets, the kaleidoscope of accents, Chinese, Italian, Australian, Greek. The sellers pass him gifts with a wink, an apple with its stalk still attached, an orange, a soft cheek of mango. Once, sugared almonds from a weekend wedding, netted and tied with white ribbon. He accepts the offerings, ignores the pity. He tucks the fruit away for the long hours ahead.

Afterwards, at the club, Michael will sometimes prop him in a seat at the poker table. Feed him lemonade until late, when Peter slips from his chair and falls asleep at his father's feet. Or he'll leave him in the car with a drink and a bag of chips until the game is won or lost. Hours. All night or into the next two days. The boy sits in the car until he's too tired or too fed up, and then he goes to his father for money for food, a drink, to beg to sit at the table and watch. The idea of gambling, of the wager, the chance, the dice, is laid down then in his memory, perhaps in his cells.

And now that they're settled in Maitland and his new network is established, Michael no longer restricts his gambling to Sydney. The spare room upstairs becomes a den where he runs a card game every week as well as a two-up 'school'. The stakes are high: he regularly sits down to Manila Poker or the Greek *Yiftiko* with a thousand pounds in his pocket. The lure of the win makes him reckless. He has a shotgun in the house, and is not averse to chasing a thief one night, with the gun and Peter in the ute beside him. He regularly wins and loses the same amount at the tables. When he wins he is all benevolence and winks, and Sophia will have new shoes. And it is a thousand pounds worth of anger he unleashes on her when he loses: she is not a good mother to his sons, she is pathetic, she doesn't take care of Peter and he runs away. It is all her fault.

She too had come from Kythera, an island drained of marriageable men. Her own brothers had fled to Australia years before; they'd urged her to join them. There were opportunities here, family, potential husbands among the men who all helped each other get jobs, find shops and flats and wives. Nothing to lose and everything to gain.

But after her marriage to Michael she finds that Maitland is far from her brothers, the family, their culture and language. So when the violence erupts she has nowhere to turn. No way to translate her feelings, no mechanism to respond with, to shed the pain. She responds instinctively, in the only way she knows – she takes out all her anger and loneliness and humiliation and fear on the only person in the house who is less powerful than she is: Peter.

It becomes a horrible, predictable circle. Michael disappears, loses at the tables, comes home and unleashes his own humiliation and fury on Sophia. She takes it and passes it on to Peter. *Cripple!* she will scream at him, *No use! Stupid!* – before she slaps him, knocking the child to the ground, sending him outside to the cold. For him, the day is often bracketed by cruelty, the teasing at school and punishments at home. If he's miserable, sick of the taunts, and runs and is caught and brought home, Michael will belt Peter first, for the misdemeanour, and then Sophia, for *not taking care of him*. Sophia, stung, will take her own revenge later, when Michael can't see, cunning and quiet and sure.

This is what Peter feels in his body but doesn't understand: that he is the bright and obvious symbol of all that is lost. He is the symbol of things that slip too easily from the strongest grasp. Michael and Sophia, variously damaged by violence and addiction and fear, need a receptacle for blame. For all the feelings they don't want to feel. And so, in a way, do the children at school he wants so much to fit in with, the children and their parents, who are all a bit afraid too. Well, it's the 1950s, everyone is afraid. There is a cold war in full swing, reds under the bed, nuclear missiles, potential enemies everywhere. People are possessive of what they've worked for, what it stands for. The untroubled houses. The dun-coloured suburbs. Uniformity, decency, rules.

The image of Peter confronts them the moment he swings into the playground on his wayward legs. To other children the calliper is frightening, it speaks of pain and ugliness and difference, and they are afraid of them all. It is, after all, a time when children born with Down Syndrome or cerebral palsy or physical or intellectual disability are often hidden away, if not in institutions then in their own homes. Though polio has been rife the calliper still attracts derision, humiliation. Somehow, people think without knowing it, he must have deserved it. In this way, the children as well as the adults remain blameless. Safe.

When Yvonne and Arne decided to throw in their lots together and to marry, they sat down and told each other their secrets. The conversation was planned: they would each tell the other their story, and each ask the other any and all of the questions that might lurk in their hearts. They would talk about their pasts, speak their answers, turn it all out into the air. And then put it all away. They would look forward, not back. Perhaps they hoped to defuse the sad facts, to remove any power they might have, with this brave conversation. Perhaps it symbolised a determination that the worst was over. That they could walk hopefully, optimistically, away from the shared past they'd created by speaking it and into their shared future. Into their new lives.

In this way the past might be mended, all the breaks and tears might knit together. There would not be a weak seam where the past might leak through. But the past always leaks through. Sometimes you don't notice, not consciously, not until years afterwards. As a child you might pick up a patina of sadness in a house where you are happy, you might note somewhere at the back of your mind that your mother doesn't smile much in photographs. But these things don't seem alarming – your mother smiles at *you*, after all, is proud of your school reports, makes your favourite food on your birthday. Sews dresses for you *and* for your dolls, ties ribbons in your hair, tucks you into bed at night. If she is sad, or impatient, if she looks grim when she hoses the garden or mixes a cake or offers a cold cheek to your father when he comes in from the workshop some nights, then you must look to yourself, try harder to be good. To be better, to be whatever it is she needs you to be. Most important: you must not disappoint her. In this you must be vigilant.

The new pregnancy is her fourth, if you count the earlier, violent miscarriage. But, of course, this time it's different. She is different, her life is re-made. Still, pregnancy has been uncertain ground for her, where all her notions of safety are contested. For the first nine months of 1956 she breathes hope and optimism, wills it to be all right. Despite her determination, it's still difficult: she's hospitalised for weeks with high blood pressure and troubled kidneys.

The child born in September will be marked by this internal weather, and by the past, present and future: the weight of a great determination that after all that has gone before, this new family will be happy, it will be whole. There are breaks and fissures in the past, things that can't be retrieved – but the squirming shape in the wicker basket in the flat is proof of what might be salvaged, what might be gained.

I am named Kristina, for my father's mother. Partly to celebrate the arrival of the first girl in his family in generations: so far this century there have been boys, with names like Bertil, Axel, August, Kjell, Lennart, Nils. Now there are two daughters.

Sunshine Number One, he calls them, and Sunshine Number Two. His dark-haired girls.

This is what Sharon remembers from this time: watching her mother's belly puff like a balloon beneath her smocks. There was a baby growing there, her mother said, a brother or sister for her. Like magic, Sharon thought. She stood sideways in front of the mirror, leaning back, poking her own belly out into roundness. *What are you doing?* Yvonne smiled, coming up behind her. *I'm having a baby sister*, Sharon replied, straining to stay upright. She's made her own decision: a girl. Later, she will know it was magic of her own that delivered her what she wanted. The baby in the basket was indeed a girl, the sister she wishes into being.

But then – it seems sudden to Sharon – everything is unsettled, her mother is always tired and snaps at her, because the baby cries all night and much of the day. An angry rash rages over her sister's face and limbs; when she is undressed for a bath Sharon can see the whole of the little body is splotched with red. She lays her head beside the baby's and blows gently on her skin, the way her father blows on her own scratches and scrapes, just a puff, to make it feel better. But nothing seems to make her sister better.

In the doctor's surgery up on Brunswick Street, Sharon watches as women in the waiting room look at her little sister and move their children away. *They think she's contagious*, her mother says evenly when she asks. *Don't take any notice. They're more contagious than she is.*

I don't remember the worst of the eczema, though apparently it lasted for years. Only the sensation of cool water, tender fingers, and the black tar ointment I can smell even now, as if it's been scooped from the road outside in summer. The impossibility of wool and soap. The consolation of dirt, on my hands and in my mouth. And the cotton clothes I played in all day and refused to relinquish at bedtime, though they were filthy with play. My second – unmarked – skin.

By late that year, they have finally saved enough money and move into the main house. The carved-off flats have left one large room that serves as kitchen, dining and living room, a bathroom and, up three wide steps, two bedrooms and a small sleep-out. There is a laundry with concrete tubs and boiler, a water tank outside, and two toilets that resemble bathing pavilions at the bottom of the yard. A vegetable garden dug into the soil along the side fence with stray dahlias poking through. A chook pen, a garage, trees. A workshop where, Yvonne suspects, her husband is happiest, where he sits or stands at a workbench, frowning or pursing his lips as he makes and mends things – small motors, household appliances, the toasters and jugs and irons that people still mend, in 1956, rather than replace.

And the shop. Another one, Yvonne might think, though they don't sell anything except batteries and fuses, sometimes a wireless or a lead. Still, it ties her; the bell erupting through the day's chores because someone can't make their toast or boil the water for tea. She'll listen to them and chat, tie a tag to the wayward appliance. Go back to the washing – she washes all the linen for the tenants, and cleans their flats – or to making a pound of mince into a meal. And sometimes, to tend to Eliza, Old Gran, who comes to stay on and off as age begins to slow her. Old Gran tells stories to Sharon, and sits beside the highchair and slips sweets into the new baby's fingers – *But*

Mimi, she croons at any protests, *look at that little face!* And dunks fresh jam drops into endless cups of tea.

Twice a day when Old Gran is staying, Yvonne kneels beside her and gently bathes the ulcers that plague the old woman's legs. This grandmother she adores, this grandmother who saved her. As the gentian violet purples her skin, Eliza looks down at her granddaughter's dark hair, the streak of grey that appeared overnight, it seems, just after Sharon was born. *You do too much, my dear*, she says. But neither of them mentions the grey.

Arne dreams his second son just before he is born in early 1959. They've been talking about the baby since the pregnancy was confirmed, confiding to each other their shy hopes for a boy. This one has been even more precarious than the others; Yvonne's body constantly threatens to miscarry the baby, or so it seems. These days her hormone levels might be tested to see if she is low in progesterone, but in 1959 the old women around her have their own ideas. *There's something wrong with that baby*, she is told, *you should run around the yard and try to lose it*. But Yvonne has her own suspicions that have nothing to do with the baby's health. And when Arne tells her his dream one early morning, hurrying out to the clothes line where she bends to pluck wet shirts from a basket, she lifts her face to him and smiles, her own feelings confirmed. *It's going to be a boy!* He's sure of it. *Yes*, she says, knowing the tenuousness, the uncertainty of the past nine months could mean only that. A son.

He is born on Easter Sunday and named Ashley. *Man from the ash forest*, that's what she's read. It's a good, strong name, she thinks, a name with strong roots; a name to fix you in place. That's what they need, a talisman to ensure their intentions.

Is the birth of this boy freighted with sadness as well as with joy? Did they both imagine the shapes of their first sons in their new one? In baby photographs Ashley has almost the same face as me; we inherit our father's bones. Seven years later, when Andrew is born, we are shocked by his difference, his face fuller than ours and beautiful even then. No doubt we see what we want to see in the faces of children, and perhaps our parents dismiss any likeness either boy might have to Peter or to Lennart, or don't mention it. Besides, this is *their* new life together. They have their pact. The past is another place and they don't live there any more.

Still, there is a part of Yvonne that the past will never leave. It accosts her every time she sees, on the street, a boy of a certain height and colouring, a boy with almond eyes. She can't control it: her heart flails about in her chest, her legs liquefy. If the boy catches her stare she turns quickly away, chides herself and the tears that spring to her eyes like this. She holds the new baby boy to her breast and throws a net of fierce love around him. Around them all.

She tightens the net hardest around Sharon, watches her like a hawk. Sharon is impulsive, determined, unafraid of consequences, but if Yvonne recognises her younger self it only toughens her resolve to shape her. Behaviour she might dismiss as amusing in another child is alarming in Sharon: the tall tales she tells at school, her casual way with rules, her preference for playing with boys. Anything to do with dishonesty – a white lie, or 'borrowing' money, as she'd once caught her doing before Ashley was born. Two shillings that belonged to Old Gran. She can remember the white heat of rage that consumed her when she came across the florin as she was making Sharon's bed. Rage, and an unidentified fear that stayed with her for hours.

For Sharon the incident is double-edged too. The two-shilling piece was just a beacon, silver-shiny and hard to ignore, there next to Old Gran's hanky, beside the hatpin with the pearly oval end. She'd walked past it, doubled back, picked it up and placed it on the flat of her palm. Rubbed an index finger around its ridges, absorbing novelty. The richness of it, the warmth. She knew Old Gran would not mind her borrowing it. Old Gran loved her, had kind eyes. She closed her fist around the shine and hurried away to hide it under her pillow, testing out the idea of ownership.

Then suddenly: her mother's face, twisted in anger. The flash of the coin in her fingers like a warning. Why hadn't she seen that before? The danger. Her mother was growling: *You are nothing but a thief.* Her voice restrained, terrifying. She took Sharon's arm gruffly and pulled her from the bedroom. *You're going to give this back and apologise*, she said.

Sharon stood before the old woman, weighed down by the word *thief.* By images of bandits in story books, handkerchiefs tied over rough faces, cruel. She thought: I am not a thief. She offered the two shillings in an outstretched hand. *I didn't steal it*, she said. She looked at Old Gran's gentle face. Was that a glint, shiny as a coin, in her papery eyes? But – *Say it,* her mother insisted, so she said it: *Sorry.* Lowered her own eyes as she walked away. Shame lodged in her then, she sees and tells me these years later, and didn't leave, a fine splinter beneath the olive skin her mother recognised and couldn't forget was Michael's.

The year Ashley is born Sharon finds her childhood calling: marbles. She'd never been much interested in hanging around with girls – *They just play basketball or walk around talking*, she says. *Boys do stuff.* Like play marbles, endlessly. One afternoon she asks if she can play and they say, *Girls can't play marbles!* But they let her, just this once, and she wins.

She starts off the season with just a few pieces, plain glass spheres, cheap. But week by week she keeps winning, and soon the boys are turning up after school to ask Mister Olsson if they can play marbles with his daughter. They arrive barefoot and full of swagger and high expectations, to do battle in the dirt patch beneath the mango tree. Big Ringsy, Little Ringsy, tracks. But they leave with empty pockets and long faces. Surprised by loss – and that a girl would not only win but keep the stash. *I don't play for fun-sy*, she explains to their retreating backs, *I play for keep-sy*. And why wouldn't she? The beautiful marbles that fall into her hands: the kingas, the blood alleys. The pee-wees and aggies. By the end of the season she has tins of them.

Watching her daughter kneel in the dirt in old shorts and a dirt-smeared blouse, her ponytail coming loose and her eyes focused murderously on the dirt ring, Yvonne sees in Sharon, or imagines, the streak of risk, the uncalculated gamble. She thinks of bloodlines – Michael mainly, but Veronica too – the strength of obsession, the tenacity of it, and she will keep tightening the rules and holds on Sharon's behaviour. Her daughter might play *for keep-sy*, but these days so does she.

Peter is ten years old, and unknowingly he is laying down a pattern for his life – running. When trouble finds him, when he is confused or hurt, this is his impulse. To escape, avoid. Movement soothes his anxiety, takes him from the landscape of his injury – home, the shop, the savagery of his father's hands or his stepmother's spite. Now she calls him *koutsos*, cripple, and his real mother *putana*, a prostitute. Her own misery has schooled her well: you feel better, she's quickly learned, if others around you feel worse.

Alone on the streets, or riding the trains, survival distracts him, hunger, cold, thirst. But these things don't bother him so much. He is never afraid out there, not the way he is at home.

Of course, it doesn't last. He is always found, an hour, a day later, by the police or by Michael who takes him home and expresses his relief and concern with a variety of implements: a strap, a piece of wet rope, a dog chain. Or the impenetrable darkness of a locked shed where, despite his silence during the beltings, Peter screams through the night. Until there are complaints from the neighbours about noise. Or the police arrive and demand his release. They stare in dismay at the boy's paralysed leg, the welts on his arms and back. But: *He is always running away. He takes money, we can't trust him*, his father says. The police write in their files, warn Peter of courtrooms and boys' homes. None of this stops Peter from running.

He is eleven. Or is he? His birthday isn't celebrated. His father is confused about the date, as he is about his own. For the boy, safety is the feel of train tracks beneath him, or parks at night, curled beneath the overhang of bushes. Old men share their scraps with him, their coats, rummage to the bottom of the rubbish bin to find him half a pie, some discarded bread. To Peter, this might feel like love. If he knew what that was.

So it doesn't seem strange, he doesn't flinch, when a man speaks to him at Luna Park, buys him a Coke, takes him back to his room in a boarding house. And the fondling, the molesting doesn't feel unkind; he doesn't like it much but he's not frightened. Not then. When the police find him a week later he shows no outward sign of trauma. On the contrary, he feels special, cared for: for a whole week he's had affection from another human being.

'. . . at interview he is a passive boy who has little self-confidence. He tells of his unhappiness because his father and stepmother seem to prefer his younger brother and how his stepmother chases or hits him when she gets annoyed. He doesn't like other boys much — they call him "Polio Pete" — and things like that. He knows it is wrong to steal but he gets so miserable he feels he has to do something so he steals and runs away. Last time he was too frightened to go home. He didn't particularly like the man who took him to his room but he had nowhere else to go and although he didn't like the man's sexual activities he didn't know what to do about it and felt it was better to stay with him than go home.

'This boy developed symptoms relating to emotional deprivation and rejection while he was away from his father during the time he developed polio. His father, who appears to work long hours in his shop, was unable to give him the support and affection which would have been necessary to overcome these symptoms and Peter felt this as his father's rejection, confirmed by his father's re-marriage to a woman who seems to have made little attempt to get him to like her. The condition was rendered more difficult by Peter's inferiority *feelings about his weak leg and his inability to cope successfully with other children.'*

The Children's Court magistrate reads the psychiatrist's report and looks down at the father and son before him. Warns Peter about running away, the dangers of strange men, and sends him outside. *You know the boy is worried because of his bad leg,* he says to the father, *and the little difficulty that is in the home between the boy and you and your present wife. Does she want the boy to come back?*

Yes.

He is an unhappy boy, the magistrate says, *and you will have to try and make him happy in the home, otherwise he will continue to run away and as he gets older he might seek out the type of man who was with him in this bedroom.*

Yes.

That type of man is willing to be kind to boys.

Yes.

Michael makes undertakings to support his son and provide him with 'sex instruction from some competent person'. Peter makes undertakings to be good. On the charge of being a neglected child, and exposed to moral danger, he is released to Michael on probation, and together they go home. An hour after walking through the door, he is gone again.

Everyone tries to paper over the sexual abuse – *I doubt if his contact with a homosexual has been of much significance to him this time*, says one report – but officially, at least, the experience changes everything. It's as if, suddenly, Peter is visible. His life turns into paper, a correspondence between police, courts, government departments, welfare agencies, hospitals, shelters and his father. Through these Peter is traced in outline, in euphemism, in the coy language of officialdom. He is *neglected*, or in *moral danger*, he is placed *on probation* and threatened with a *training school*. He *absconds* and is *apprehended*, again and again and again, and told finally that, if he *breaches* one time too many, he will be *committed to the care of the Minister*.

Only one document hints at the real child behind the words, his innocence, his fear, his misery – Peter was vulnerable to paedophiles at the time, it says, because he was *on the run, in need of shelter, a timid, suggestible boy lacking in self-assertion*. But he is nonetheless *cheerful, pleasant and respectful*. The language of his official life ducks and weaves as effectively as Peter does around his own pain.

When Old Gran comes to stay there are always visitors. Everyone loves the preparation almost more than the event. The night before, the old lady carefully winds her fine grey hair around strips of cotton and pins them in place. Then the cold cream, scraped over her face like icing on a cracked cake. For the children, leaning against a nearby wall, the effect is at once terrifying and hysterical. They don't know whether to laugh or cry, but are saved from both when Old Gran turns her head and calls out: *Put out my good dress will you, Mimi? And my stays. And a clean hanky, love.*

In the morning, Yvonne mixes eggs and milk and flour for pikelets as Old Gran *titivates* in front of a mirror. That's what she says if anyone asks her what she's doing. She rubs rouge into papery cheeks, presses on lipstick. Unpins the wisps of hair. And then, in a cloud of lavender talcum powder, she coos and talks to the baby while he is bathed. He's placed in her lap while Yvonne changes her dress and the girls are coaxed into clean clothes. There's a sweet for Sharon if she's been good: if she's played with her sister, helped her mother with the baby's bath – even if she's chanced it and asked once more if she can do up the nappy pin, and once more been told *No*.

Sometimes the visitors are Val and her children; they've moved into one of the flats on the other side of the wall. Everyone loves Val, her undefeated cheerfulness, her vivacity. If there are others – Val's own sisters, or Yvonne's – they all end up in the downstairs kitchen warming milk for cocoa and playing cards. Yvonne loves these nights. The easy company of other women, the innocent pleasure of talk and story and jokes, the big family feel of it. They make toast and it isn't long before Old Gran says, *What about a song, my dears?* Val and her sisters grin, leap to their feet and dance the cancan, singing and whooping. Everyone claps and laughs. At the end they turn and flip up their skirts, and Old Gran feigns outrage. *Oh my dears!* she says. And as soon as they stop she pleads with them to do it again.

Every now and then, the front flat becomes home to one of Yvonne's siblings – Ann and her husband, or Laurie and his wife. To them she is the parent who never judges or criticises, who will help with a baby or a toddler or with a meal if they're broke. That's what they'll remember: she'll do anything she can for them. For anyone. Ann has never forgotten the baby her sister had brought home to Cannon Hill, and then mysteriously lost, the little boy she cuddled and loved and whose name Veronica forbade them all to speak. She'd felt, as a child, that she had lost him too. So when her own son is born these years later, while she is living in the front flat, Ann brings him to her big sister and shyly says she wants to call him *Peter*.

She lies awake with darkness lapping at tired eyes. Exhaustion heavy in her limbs. He is part of the weight tonight, her first son. In her waking dreams he has shape-shifted; from happy baby to coddled child to angry young man who hates her, hates her. And back again, back to what she dreads most, the boy lost. She tries to blink it all away but so many nights this boy lies down with her, clawing at her heart. *What if* is the refrain, *what if.* A soft tearing sound.

In the morning she will begin again. She will set out breakfast cereal, milk, spoons, she will tie shoelaces and hair ribbons, cut sandwiches in neat triangles for lunchboxes. Peel oranges, winding the skin back on for their schoolbags. She will tidy, wipe faces clean, floors, plates. Set vegetables to soak for dinner. Loop clothes along a washing line in white midday sun; mix eggs and milk for custard. Her hands can never be busy or full enough. Despite what they do and what they hold, pegs, dishes, laundry, soap, she can still feel the precise shape and weight of a child, thirteen months old. His limbs circling her. The phantom at her hip.

December is the worst. Heat accumulates in her body as the eighteenth approaches. She tries to hide her preoccupation. *It's just Christmas*, she'll say if someone asks. *Too much to do.* On the day, she washes and cooks and purses her lips hard over all they threaten to release: words, a name, the cry that will undo her. Commemoration.

Some years she will allow herself this: his baby photograph. A wish. Even the courage of speaking: *Today*, she'll say, *he'll be ten, eleven, twelve*, to her husband or her sister as they sit at the table with their tea. No more is necessary, only a hand on her back, on her arm. The unspoken hangs between them – *I wonder if, how, where*. And the longing, endless, palpable.

Sometimes the weight, the exhaustion of carrying it, is too much. This is such a day, despite the sun after endless rain, and children running in the yard – Ashley, Andrew, little boys from the neighbourhood – despite the satisfaction of clean white sheets on the line. She breathes them in: for her it's the smell of salvation – clean washing, scrubbed lino, cotton pressed hot by the iron. From the hoist she can see women in other backyards heaving washing into the sunshine, or bending to pull weeds from damp soil. Sometimes this gladdens her, the communal rituals of women. But not today. She turns back into the laundry, an ache building within her.

She pummels clothes in the concrete tubs and readies them for the wringer, twisting and flattening and guiding them through the rollers. At least once her fingers gain traction and she reefs them out with seconds to spare. There have been days when she wasn't so nimble, the rollers catching and bruising her fingers, black and blue. She'd been grateful they weren't broken.

Outside, the boys' game has built to a crescendo. They shriek like banshees, a wild sound, and she can tell they're running, from the breathless laughs, louder and louder. She steps outside to check on them. And catches her own breath. There on the line, on the spanking white sheets: the travesty of mud, great gobs of it. As she watches, a boy hurls another; it smacks against fabric. They all screech, hysterical with the joy and terror of it; they run, bend to scoop mud and run again, hurling it at each other and missing, their filthy little faces alight. There's the slap of wet earth against skin and wet cotton.

The weight in her shifts dangerously. She's quickly upon them, barely aware she's moved at all. Aware only of this sullying, this rampant carelessness. She shouts at the neighbours' boys to *get home*. Their faces whiten beneath the dirt and they vanish. As they do, Ashley slips beneath the low stumps of the workshop and Andrew follows. Their fear, the shaking in their skinny, dirt-crusted legs does nothing to diminish her rage.

They'll never forget it: their mother – her face, her whole person, transfigured. Screaming at them to come out, it will be worse if they don't. The belting she delivers with hands she's lost control of, or that's how it seems, the red welts that stay on their legs for hours. And this: their own distress, not just at the rare punishment, and their mother's face, but at the tears that stream down her cheeks as she smacks them, the tears that match theirs. Later, remembering, they'll both wonder who hurt the most.

By now the children sense the sadness that tightens their mother's face so many mornings; they sense but cannot know the subterranean emotions and the pain. So they do what many children do when they're confused: they take her pain as their own. Because surely, if she is unhappy, it is something to do with them. If something is wrong, they must have done it. So all they can do now is make up for it somehow, for what they've done or haven't done, what they are or aren't enough of.

They don't know how close this is to the truth. They *aren't* enough. When you have five children and there are only four beneath your roof, running about the yard, then four is not enough. I wonder now that she didn't explode more often. Not just in the privacy of her home but outside, at the corner shop, the doctor's surgery, in the street, anywhere there were children and idle conversation and someone blithely asked her: *And how many children do you have?* The betrayal of numbers, whatever her reply.

They've given Peter one more chance, a month's trial at home — *I promise I will not run away again and I will go to school*, he says, and tries to mean it. But a week later he's escaped the schoolyard and is found that night at Collaroy station. His father is furious and the police have lost their patience. When he hears the magistrate say the words *ward of the State* and *Weroona*, Peter's stomach flips with a mix of relief and fear. And the confusion of his ragged love for his father, his yearning for somewhere to belong. A home, but different from his own, which is measured in misery and heartache, blow by blow.

So Peter is unsettled by his first institution, surprised by safety. By belonging. It is like the home he has in dreams: there is order here, discipline, but there is also kindness. A sense of the world as fair. Schoolwork and pot-scrubbing and cricket and marbles. The gift of a prayer book, never to be lost. A trip to town every fortnight with a shilling to spend. For the first time he can remember, there is nothing to run away from, no reason to steal.

'Weroona', in the clean air of the Blue Mountains, is comparatively benign. We might be grateful for institutions like this one – though it's a prison of sorts, a child's prison – but for this: what they say about the world outside them. Weroona will be the first of several institutions to shelter Peter through his turbulent adolescence – not all so modest in their approach – but if he feels safe in them, no longer alone, surely this indicts us all. That we live happily knowing a child feels better and safer in a prison than he does in the houses and streets outside it.

The above-mentioned lad has been at Weroona for the past eight months. During this period he has been a good type of lad who appears very contented here. He is well mannered, keeps himself clean and tidy and mixes well with the other boys . . . If he is restored to his father in the near future it will have to be impressed on his father that Peter is still a child and that he is too immature to be made to accept the responsibility of looking after any of his business ventures . . . although Peter is nearly twelve he still looks for a lot of guidance from adults when he attempts any undertaking or task . . . (November 1960)

Since his committal Peter has settled down very well. He has never absconded or indulged in any thieving which was his main failing whilst he was living with his father and stepmother. He has gained self-assurance, but still looks to adults for guidance in many respects. He is a boy who shows interest in the home and likes to carry out many little duties in the garden . . . (June 1961)

The manager feels that the lad could now be restored to his father provided that home conditions are suitable, as the lad has reached the stage of self-confidence that he previously lacked. When the father called at Head Office he was warned of the lad's inability to work weekends and nights in the shop. He then suggested he would defer his application until the end of this year. Although Peter is only twelve and a half years of age, it could be that his father sees in him a source of cheap labour . . . (July 1961)

But Michael does not defer his application, and Peter is home late in August, 1961. By the first week of October, he is truanting again, a few shillings from the till and he's off to Luna Park, or just riding the trains, around and around. Somewhere in his head he is looking for another Weroona. He didn't really want to leave; he liked everyone there and they liked him. He even liked the schoolroom. But at the state school in Liverpool, as at home, he is a *wog*, and a *cripple*, a *peg-leg* – though he craves inclusion with the boys who taunt him, almost grateful for the attention. Better not to go to school at all, he decides, to stick to the streets. Here he may not feel loved, exactly, but he finds that everyone is like him: misfits, drop-outs, the sad and forgotten. They recognise him as one of their own. It's true that occasionally he's nervous but he's never angry and hurt, the way he is at home. His father tells him he'll be found dead on the streets one day, but that doesn't deter him or scare him. He would never tell his father if he *was* scared.

There is a brief period of calm when he pretends to the visiting authorities that everything is fine, he won't run away again and he tries, truly, to be good. He works hard in his father's hamburger shop, standing on a crate to reach the milkshake machine. But he can't bear the violence that erupts like a ripe boil in the house, and when he feels its approach he flees. It's back to the old pattern. Police, courts, disappearances, the fury of his father and stepmother. There are warnings and reports and beltings, nights sleeping in sheds and trains and the protective arms of shrubs under the Harbour Bridge. When the police and social workers ask him why, he doesn't have an answer. Especially if his father is there. There's the cruelty of home and school but sometimes, as he walks alone at night or hauls his calliper up into a train carriage, he feels he's not so much running away as running towards.

This is what he doesn't know: that even before polio condemned him to pain and humiliation, his body was imprinted with his mother's, and with her absence. Unconsciously, his body registers all that is missing: any feeling of love or attachment from his father and stepmother, every bruise and cruelty they inflict as they project the anger and pain of their own lives. He is a child, still. An adult might understand the actions of other adults, or try to, but to a child already suffering *emotional deprivation and rejection*, as his psychiatrist writes, the abuse at home and at school can only confirm his solitary station in the world, his otherness.

The one notion that pulls him through, like a bright thread he can follow in the dark, is that somewhere, he has a real mother. A woman just like those he sees with other boys, someone a bit like his aunt, Adriana: someone warm, kind, someone who cooks cakes and sings in the kitchen and who smells good, of talcum powder and eau de cologne. Who waits for him to come home from school, who ruffles his hair and jokes with him as Sophia does with George, and helps him with the spelling he still can't seem to do, and still kisses him goodnight, even now that he's big.

He knows this other mother, this *real* one, exists somewhere, though his father refuses to speak of her, dismissing Peter's questions with a wave of his hand or a slap and *she ran away, she didn't want you*. But Peter knows better. He doesn't believe any of the insults Michael and Sophia fling around about her. He *knows*. It all adds to the vague picture forming in his head. From somewhere, he has no idea where, he has heard the name *Yvonne*. He imagines a young, pretty French girl with a chignon and dainty hands. Even if she did run away, he refuses to believe she ran away from *him*. From Michael, perhaps, and from the miserable life they lead, he can understand that.

He begins to see they have much in common, his lovely French mother and him. One day he'll get away for good too.

Their mother watches, knows their days.

There are children in the mango tree. Limbs against limbs, skin on bark. They are hiding, or they are presiding, or they are reading or fighting, among the hot green and leaves singing. It is summer, their chins and fingers run with mango juice. They climb, they splay over branches, hands and feet reaching for safety – they are testing solidity, a sticky embrace.

Or: they are running, tree to tree – mulberry, locquat, banana – sliding narrow bodies between garage and fence, pressed between fibro and choko vine. A sibling or a cousin is counting, *eight, nine, ten, coming ready or not.* She sees a shiver ruffle through them, it might be the game, the hiding, or the proximity of grasshoppers. They hate grasshoppers.

Or: they are on the wide expanse of grass between trees and washing line and the outside toilets. It's still summer. They are playing rounders but they are dreaming, each of them: of the bay where they're taken to swim each Christmas and Easter in flat salty water, or the bicycles they crave but aren't allowed to have. Or the biscuits their mother might be baking, now that the washing is pegged and slapping on the line, the vegetables peeled and soaking in their pots, the kitchen swept.

Perhaps, if it's late afternoon, they are under rather than within the mango's high skirt, in a patch of soft earth, pushing marbles or toy cars down finger-wide tracks. *Castle*, she hears one murmur, pressing a thumb-print beside her. *Garage*, says another with a Matchbox ute. Green, like his father's. He drops tiny sticks into the tray – they are electrical wire, cords, leads. He looks towards the house, the driveway, waiting for the growl of an engine. Waiting for when he can say it: *Dad's home*, and they race to get there first.

Watching them from behind kitchen louvres, their mother might allow contentment to briefly wash over her. She is, after all, the guardian of all they dream. She might allow the deep love she has for them to surface, to tingle in her fingers and hands and for her heart to feel itself full. She might wish she could simply say it, tell her children – her husband too – how much she loves them, run out into the yard and embrace them. But finds she cannot. Instead she turns to the jam drops cooling on the bench, the potatoes peeled and ready for boiling, the school clothes fresh from the line – her love implicit in each press of the iron, each curl of vegetable peel, each word of praise for homework well done or a kindness shown by one to another. In each new shirt or dress she cuts and sews for them, each ribbon she ties, each story she tells. Even in the discipline meted out. She knows these, and not empty expressions or extravagant demonstrations, are the real work of love.

It is an ordinary-looking day some time in 1963. Sharon is drinking cordial in the kitchen when Arne walks in, tells her he wants to talk to her in his office. A summons to the office, adjacent to the shop at the front of the house, is rare, and usually presages a serious talk, or a dressing down. At thirteen Sharon has had many of these, so as he turns away she scours her memory for any misdeeds or mischief she's guilty of. It could be any number of things. She takes a deep breath and follows her father out of the room.

The office has two big wooden desks, walls of shelving and sets of filing cabinets.

On his desk, the one near the window to the driveway, there is a long black bakelite telephone that receives calls and transfers them to the workshop in the backyard, where he spends hours after work repairing appliances. There's a Swedish Helvetia typewriter, a wide blotter, paper, pens, trays, a spike for bills paid and messages received. The other desk has books, manuals, and the heavy job diary his foreman writes in every day. It smells of paper and ink, of books, of serious things recorded and kept.

But for Sharon the office smells mostly of trouble. She wanders in to find her father at his desk – a place where business is done, transactions are made – in an ancient swivel chair. He motions Sharon to the seat facing him. He says, *I want to have a talk to you.* Then smiles tentatively. He has a way of composing himself when he has something important to say, as if he is at a lectern. Even if it's an audience of one. He clears his throat, adopts a thoughtful, narrative tone. In this way, he often turns announcements into stories.

Sharon watches as he does these things, readying himself. She thinks: *It can't be too bad,* but she can't relax yet. His displeasure can be hidden behind such smiles and such tones. He clears his throat again. *You know,* he begins, *that I'm not your legal father* – a hesitation over the words to come – *your biological father. Your other father's name is on your birth certificate.*

Sharon thinks wildly about the word *biological* before it clicks into place in her head. His accent has made it exotic, strange. She nods.

Well, he says and pauses again, pressing his lips together. *I would like to legally adopt you. To be your legal father.* A simple sentence, a stone dropped into a pool. But she's struggling with the sound of it, the Swedish inflection thicker somehow now, and she realises he's nervous too.

In the pause he looks at the floor, the patterned brown lino, then up again. *It's been my plan for a long time. But I wanted to wait until you were old enough to decide for yourself. To decide if that's what you want.*

Sharon stares at him. These sentences, these ideas. It's quiet here in the room, she can hear muffled noises from the kitchen, a cup placed on a saucer, footsteps to and fro, but still she feels as if they – she and he – have been picked up and dropped in a different country. She has two immediate reactions: relief that she isn't in trouble after all, and a kind of confusion. What is it exactly he is asking her to decide?

He goes on. *You would have a new birth certificate. The other name would be rubbed out. You would be Sharon Olsson, officially.* He purses his lips over the *sh* sound; she loves it when he does that. *Just like now, but legal.* He stresses the word *legal*, as if it's in capital letters. *That's very important, especially if anything happens to me. You are one of my children, just like the others.* Then that smile. *But it's up to you. If that's what you want.*

In one definite heartbeat Sharon understands completely. *Like the others. Legal.* But there's no decision to be made; that was done years before. Perhaps on those picnics in sunlit fields, or on the long drives, sitting between them, or perhaps in some unknown moment where it all accumulated, every word and gesture of fatherliness, every lecture and smack and ruffling of her hair, every puff of breath on a scraped knee, every query about maths homework and click of his camera on her birthdays.

So: *You've always been my father*, she says, and shrugs, as if she's answering a too-easy algebra question. A lop-sided smile. *And that's what I want.*

She sits looking at him. There's the taste of orange cordial in her mouth. *Well*, he says, and she hears the crack in his voice. Once again he presses his lips together. *That's good. I'll see to it then. The documents.* There's nothing left to say. She'd like to get outside now, to let the words settle, to test out this new skin. So she goes to him and hugs him. He pats her head and says, *Good girl*, and sends her on her way. She walks straight down to the mango tree and starts to climb. The rough bark, the view from the top over chook-pen and yard, feels at once familiar and altered, utterly. The papers are deposited with lawyers and Yvonne and Arne wait to hear if Sharon's biological father will acknowledge her, fight the adoption or deny her. It takes months, but it's unambiguous: Michael Preneas raises no objection to the adoption. Arne Olsson is Sharon's legal father.

But Michael is never entirely obliterated. He hovers behind every episode of trouble Sharon finds herself in: the stories she makes up to tell her friends and teachers; the fights in the playground; the rules she waives against walking home from school via back laneways; the mouthy girls she loiters with, the bullies she pushes into the local pool. At high school she is caught smoking, forgets her homework, but distinguishes herself mainly by swallowing mercury for a dare in chemistry class. She hasn't counted on an ambulance ride and a near-death experience, and the threat of expulsion when she recovers. Those boys didn't know who they were daring, she tells her parents later, and Yvonne, appalled, marches her to the principal's office to apologise.

Then there are the flights from home. Yvonne is surprised and perturbed when, the first time Sharon runs away, it is Ronnie she runs to. She wonders if her mother has encouraged the girl somehow, worries about her influence. Yvonne doesn't realise how comfortable Sharon is in Ronnie's company, that she feels more like a young friend of her grandmother than a child, because Ronnie talks to her without a warning in her voice. That first time the child ran, Ronnie found her in the afternoon, crouching in the dirt under the house, a bag of bread and butter in her hand, a forlorn look on her face. She roused on her good-naturedly then took the girl upstairs. *You and I are kindred spirits*, she said, grinning. *We're just gay dogs.*

So later, when Sharon begins to feel curious about the man on her birth certificate, she takes her questions to Ronnie. She knows she can't ask her mother; *her* past is a locked vault. Sharon takes the bus to Cannon Hill, ostensibly to hang around with Wendy, but doesn't leave Ronnie's side all afternoon. Finally she fields her question: *What was my real father like?* They're in the kitchen; she watches as her grandmother plunges a knife through a Queensland Blue. She loves Ronnie's strong, stubby fingers, her competent hands. There's a crack as the pumpkin's thick skin gives beneath the blade.

A mongrel. Sharon is surprised by the growl in Ronnie's voice. *Beat her black and blue. Worked her like a slave and then left her to starve.* A wedge of creamy yellow pumpkin falls from the whole. Ronnie grips the knife with one hand and balances the pumpkin with the other. *Gambled every penny. And your mother in ragged underwear, bras that didn't fit.*

Ronnie takes the vegetables to the stove and empties them into a pot.

What was his name? Sharon says to her back.

Her grandmother turns, twists her hands in a tea-towel. Hesitates. Then, *Michael*, she says, and her voice twists too, she almost spits the word. *Mick.*

And Sharon opens her mouth to say *What else?* as Ernest walks into the room.

But later, before dinner, she follows Ronnie around the kitchen saying *Tell me more about him*, as Ronnie stirs a custard and checks the stew. *Tell me about Mum.* This is how she learns that her mother went away on a train and got into trouble. That her father is a Greek bastard and a womaniser and if her mother had owned a gun she would have shot him. That he pushed her down a high set of stairs, and how, pregnant with Sharon, she made her escape from him. *Don't you tell your mother I told you*, Ronnie hisses, waving a wooden spoon. *She'd have my guts for garters.*

Ronnie finishes this elided version, in which Sharon is an only child, with *He didn't want you; Greek men are only interested in sons*, and sends Sharon off to call the others in for tea. The words reverberate through Sharon all during dinner and for weeks after. *He didn't want you*. Then they fade for a while, and when she recounts them as an adult she will see they had the effect her grandmother intended: for a long time she didn't think about Michael at all. But she would never forget the images that fell from the knife with the crescents of pumpkin, and always she will see the word *bastard* in startling yellow.

On a hot day in the previous December, Yvonne had opened the door to her bedroom to find Sharon cross-legged on the floor in front of the dresser, a photograph in her hand. She couldn't see it properly from the doorway, but there was only one possibility: the photo she kept tucked beneath her petticoats and bras in the drawer now open before her daughter. Sharon looked up at her, wide-eyed, caught fair and square. A fork of anger struck Yvonne's gut. *What are you doing?* she snapped.

Sharon blinked and opened her mouth but there was no smart excuse, as there usually was when she was in a scrape. Yvonne stepped into the room. *What are you doing in that drawer?* She watched her daughter's face register the dilemma and measure a range of responses before settling on the truth. *Looking for Christmas presents*, she said meekly, and shrugged. Then looked down at her hands. *I found this.* Proffering the photo. A pause, a beat that allowed the guilelessness of Sharon's words to dilute Yvonne's rage. And for Sharon to decide there wasn't much to lose. *Who is it?* she asked.

Perhaps it was shock, or confusion, but Yvonne's anger was replaced by a surge of sadness and tears. She had to swallow before she could speak. She took a breath, leaned forward and took the photo from her daughter's hand, surprising them both with gentleness. Then subsided onto the edge of the bed, looked into her daughter's eyes.

We'll talk about this now, just this once, she said quietly, *and then never again. It's not fair on your father to raise it again.* She paused, drew another breath. *This is your brother*, she said.

Confusion clouded Sharon's face. *Ashley?* In her tone the knowledge it couldn't be, wasn't him.

Yvonne turned her head from side to side. *No. You have a brother*, she said carefully, *from my first marriage.* Stopped. Then: *His name is Peter.*

Where is he?

I don't know where he is. He's with his father. Every word serrated now. So she rushed out the rest, only what was necessary: *He's Greek. He's been raised in the Greek way, different from you. Different from your sister and brother. He'll have everything he wants, everything.* She looked past Sharon to the windows that opened out onto the yard. *He'll be just like his father.*

Now that she'd said them, the words felt right. That's what the lawyer had said, those years ago: Peter would have everything. She realised she'd leaned on that, convincing herself, ever since. And of course he'd be like his father, this first-born Greek boy, brought up in his image, with all of his ways. She put the thought away.

You'll say nothing of this to the others, she said, turning back to Sharon. *That was another life. We've got a new life now.* She managed a half-smile. *And your father has been good to you.* She stood then and motioned Sharon towards the door. *We won't talk about this any more.* Closing it off. She put a hand on her daughter's shoulder as they left the room and went down the steps to the kitchen. *Meatloaf tonight*, she said, going to the fridge. It was Sharon's favourite.

This is how Yvonne remembers it eighteen months later, watching Sharon with the new baby, her last, another almond-eyed boy. He is the kind of beautiful, robust baby everyone falls for on first sight, and rudely healthy. *What could be wrong with Andrew?* the local doctor scoffs if the baby is presented to him with a minor complaint. *That boy could eat prickly pear.* At sixteen, Sharon is devoted to Andrew, running to his every cry, propping him on her hip as she walks about the house, singing him to sleep. There are nights when Yvonne realises, as she sweeps the kitchen before bed, that she's barely had her hands on Andrew all day, that Sharon has fed and bathed him and played with him and that, grateful for the break, she's filled her hours with chores, the baby in her peripheral vision.

Still, she feels anxious about Andrew, some vague disquiet. From the beginning she'd been startled by his difference from the others; he is more like her in the shape of his face and his eyes, the jet-black hair. But watching Sharon with him, and remembering the day in the bedroom, awareness arrives abruptly. Peter, Sharon, Andrew: her last child bears an uncanny resemblance to her first. She thinks of Sharon's love for this baby, the way she attends to him, and wonders if, unconsciously, Sharon knows it too.

Around the same time, Peter is in his father's garage, cleaning. It's a long, boring job, but it's worth the few quid Michael has promised, and it's better than sitting around. Dust is sifted over every surface, old wasp casings shattered through the accumulated debris of his father's life. There are receipts for tins of oil and cases of soft drink, newspapers in Greek and English. Paperwork for the shops his father has bought and sold.

And then, suddenly, treasure. Not money or gold but better, the thing he's been looking for all his life. He sits on a box and looks at it again to make sure. His heart is making a racket in his chest. But he knows somewhere deep inside himself that the wad of paper in his hands – plain, indifferent looking – is all about his mother.

Yvonne Frances Preneas, nee Ball. It's the name he's heard before, somewhere in his countless dealings with police and social workers. But that was just a name, black and white; this is a bit of colour. It tells him where she was born, when she married his father, and even better, her maiden name.

He sits staring at the writing. *Yvonne.* He's still in love with the name, with all it implies about her, about him. And then he realises there are more papers beneath this one. He shuffles the new page to the top.

He has to read it twice before comprehension begins to build, and slowly, almost unconsciously, he rises to his feet. There is another name, *Sharon Elaine Preneas*, and a birth date, March, 1950, fifteen months after his own. *Mother, Yvonne Preneas. Father, Michael Preneas. Custody granted to mother.* The penny drops suddenly and it hits his heart. My sister, he thinks. I have a sister. He grips the piece of paper and his eyes lift to the dingy walls of the shed. Dust, dislodged by movement, ancient, drifts in the stale air. Two emotions rear up: anger and joy. He grips the wad of paper in a tight fist and hurtles crookedly into the house.

Of course, his father denies it.

Look. Peter thrusts the pages towards him. *Here's the proof. She's a year younger than me, she's got your name.*

Michael has his ear cocked to the radio; he listens for the race result, swears. Looks at his son, unperturbed. *Forget it*, he says, and turns back to the radio. *Your mother was on the streets. That kid could be anyone's kid.*

You're lying. Peter stares at his father, sees the lie on his face, and realises something important: nothing Michael says can change this sudden and wonderful knowledge. *Sharon.* The very notion of a sister is like a gift, something he doesn't have to share. He goes into the small bedroom he sometimes sleeps in and sits on the edge of the single bed. Lets it all wash over him again. Then he stores it away in his memory, to bring out now and then for reassurance and for hope. Somewhere, he has a real mother *and* a real sister. Like just about everyone else he knows.

He is an arrow, flying clean and true. Unimpeded in its flight, barely visible. But straight to its mark, from a beautiful pliant bow. This is what he dreams.

Weroona, Daruk. The pattern deepens, expands. He's a youth now with a child's emotions, a child's heart that beats the same tune, repeating it over and over: steal, run, hide. Look in the mirror: it's still the same person – peg-leg, crip, wog; unlovely, unlovable, unloved. *Love me*, his reflection says. Begs.

He asks for nothing else. No dispensations or allowances – no pity – he wants no acknowledgement of his difference at all. He drags his leg around the appalling grounds of his prisons as if his body is not damaged at all. As if he isn't. Forced marches, fist fights, attempted escapes: he's just one of the boys.

The State agrees. He is in their care; his body is theirs. They occasionally swoop and swap his institutions, a disciplinary one for a medical one. They lay him out on cold, narrow tables where he lies, naked and shivering, as doctors and students poke and prod and pronounce him ripe for intervention, for experiment. Over successive years he regularly endures the horrors of their benevolence: attempts to lengthen tendons, or his entire leg, to graft bone and sinew. There are injuries and infections, his meek skin tears and his blood clots disastrously. The pain, even to a boy inured to suffering, is insufferable. He only cries at night. By day there is the oblivion of Physeptone, toxic and addictive, but sweet. Hallucinatory. He is an arrow.

He has been slated for a stretch in Daruk Training school, where he *would benefit from the strict disciplinary training* and psychiatric treatment. But he is there for just a month when a doctor at Sydney Hospital examines his right leg and decides *the boy's condition could be considerably improved.* It is March, 1963, and for the rest of the year and into the next he will see only hospitals, operating theatres, convalescent homes and after-care facilities.

After the first surgery, when the pain has settled, there is once more the terrifying notion of walking again. But his legs are unfamiliar to him; they crumple as soon as the nurse lets go. He tries again: his brain and his body won't cooperate: they have forgotten what walking is. Day after day he tries and fails and falls. Tries not to cry. It doesn't matter if he does: no one comes to help him. Getting himself up is part of the recovery, but it is beyond his comprehension now. Nothing makes sense. He can see himself walking, he can feel himself walking. Time and again he instructs his legs to move forward. Still he falls.

There is one consolation: a bright new friendship with a boy whose back has been broken and his legs paralysed in an accident. He is the same age as Peter. His injuries have numbed all his joy and optimism along with his legs, but he and Peter joke with each other from their beds across the ward, teasing the good-looking nurses. They recognise that they are the same, across the pain and confusion and bleakness. It is a brotherhood of suffering.

But this boy has a secret, something even Peter doesn't know. Peter will only realise the depth of his friend's despair when, one night, he calls their favourite nurse to his bedside. Twists his torso around to open a drawer beside him, pulls out a cigarette packet. Peter watches the nurse, her wide eyes as she flips the packet open: it is full of pills, meticulously saved over months for one exact moment, one brave gulp.

Then Peter hears him say, *I don't need these now.* He winks at Peter across the room. A wan smile. The nurse carries the pills away.

It takes Peter some time to work it all out, the pills, his friend's declaration, the wink. When meaning finally dawns he hugs it to him, cherishing it. It's something to do with him. Perhaps – perhaps – his presence in this room, just being here, is of value to someone. Perhaps he's helped save someone's life. He is an arrow.

Cairns is Peter's magnetic north. Its pull is embedded in him, and strongest in December, the month of his birthday and the family rituals of Christmas. The month when people go home. As the rehab centre empties his eyes follow the retreating backs of people with parents, with siblings. He thinks, *Cairns, then*. The place he was born. Even the sound of it is talismanic. He decides to hitchhike up the coast and a friend from rehab with a badly broken arm says he'll come too.

It takes them days, nearly a week, of back-cracking rides in trucks and cars over sixteen hundred miles. The journey is rougher for them than it might be for others: his mate's arm is in plaster from the shoulder down and Peter has a full-length plaster cast on his right leg. He's using crutches again to get around. They make a fine pair, standing on the side of the highway, their hopeful faces turned to the roar of bitumen and engines. They use their good limbs and their bloody-mindedness to haul themselves up into the high cabs of the trucks.

But Peter has brought with him all his childlike optimism. Cairns isn't just somewhere on a map, but a place where he might look for his mother and, without records or any knowledge of his history, magically find her. Just cast about and she'll be there. In the charged air of Cairns, he might pass her in the street and know her. She'll know him. In his head, all these things are possible. He walks into the town of his birth searching the eyes of women – he'll know her by her eyes, they'll be like his. But in the sweltering streets, under monsoon skies, there is no response.

Into the vacuum, waiting for opportunity, Peter's shame comes creeping. He's not good enough to have a mother. Not good enough to be found. Probably as bad as his father says he is: a thief, a low-life, stupid, bad. He regards himself: ill-shaped, uneducated, unlovable. What father would want him? What mother? Not even Sophia! A thought strikes like a slap: they're better off without him. Michael won't belt her now that he is gone, the rough sandpaper between them. It is all his fault.

So when osteomyelitis strikes him again just after he turns seventeen, and the doctor at a Sydney hospital asks for next of kin, he won't say. He tells no one about the illness except Keith Smith, a boy he's befriended on the streets. For some reason, he finds Keith there beside him when he is admitted to hospital; he just won't go away. So it is Keith who hears the surgeons say that, this time, Peter is likely to lose his leg. They use the word *amputate*. The infection is severe, he's neglected it. Part of him wishes Keith would leave; he wants no one to see his fear or to see the hateful tears. But Keith, a quiet boy, quietly refuses. He sits with him until he goes to theatre, saying nothing except

You'll be right, mate, often enough to make Peter believe he won't be. He doesn't care; he can't wait for the anaesthetic, he wants an end to the pain. He goes to sleep with the word *amputation* going around and around in his head.

A blink of an eye and he is in the recovery room, dozing, waking. Feels for his leg. It's still there. So is Keith. *How are you, mate?* Keith says, expressionless. The sight of him as reassuring as the limb still – amazingly – attached to his body. His surgeons warn him he'll need his crutches and he'll need care. They mean the care of parents, he knows this, a tender mother to nurse him, in a home as clean as an operating theatre.

The day he is discharged he leaves the despised wooden crutches at the hospital door. Leans on Keith's shoulder and hops to the car. *I'll drive*, he says in a tone that won't brook an argument. And he does, all the way back to the boarding house he lives in, using one of his old walking sticks to push the accelerator.

His last detention is the worst, the merciless Mt Penang where he is thrown in with cruel, confused boys convicted of rape and assault. But as the resident *wog cripple* he is a rung below them, in their eyes, and once again a convenient receptacle for their pain.

He escapes the sexual violence, as well as some of the more grotesque punishments – perhaps his disability saves him – but this unusual luck doesn't exclude him from the ordinary bullying of his fellows, the casual, unpredictable punches that drop him to the ground, the thrashings. He is impervious to the pain but humiliation bites, the old reminder of his place. He feels something harden in his veins.

At night, he lies awake and tries to not to hear the sounds that come from nearby beds. The boys cry out as they are being abused, an odd noise like the calling of cats. That's what they are called. Their sheets stink of urine, and in the mornings they are made to stand by their beds, holding their wet sheets before them. Peter tries not to look at their faces, their humiliation and rage.

He doesn't know it yet, but he has stepped into the crucible. He watches as the discipline handed out to others breaks them, over and over, until they try to escape and are sent north to the notorious Tamworth detention centre. They return barely recognisable; cringing, pathetic, but full of a subterranean hatred. They remind Peter of abused dogs. Most wait out their time until they are eligible for Long Bay, where they know life is easier. He won't follow them. Swears now he will never, ever be locked up again, will never endure the cruelty. Not in these places, and not at home.

But when he resumes his life back on the streets, it speaks of what he hasn't escaped: self-loathing. He runs with a gang in Manly, picking fights for them – a casual stab of his walking stick in the beer glass of the enemy and he ducks away. Still under-age – even he thinks he's over eighteen – he gets his first tattoos. *In Memory of Mother*, and *Death Before Dishonour.* There is an eagle too, wings arched and ready for flight. He has inscribed on his flesh the three concepts that drive him: mother, honour, flight. As if they can no longer be buried, these drivers, nor contained inside his body, they erupt on his skin. He has alchemised the shame and anger, distilling them into ink.

Everyone – police and social workers, Peter himself – assumes he is a year older than he is. Michael, functionally illiterate, has either forgotten his son's age and has no way of checking, or had long ago put it up a year for his own purposes, when he had needed full-time help in the shop.

But after Mt Penang, Peter will never live with his father again. He prefers the deep shadows of the Harbour Bridge, the leafy shelters of the homeless. These are his familiars, the men with their rough speech, the metallic smell of urine and alcohol. Despite everything – infections in his leg, malnutrition – he will not go home. Michael will only parade his predictions – that Peter is useless, a bum and a derelict, that he'll die on the streets. But the streets are safer than many places Peter knows.

Then two things happen. Two things to turn a life around. After weeks of sleeping rough around the city, Peter meets the Reverend Barney Gook from St Barnabas Church in Broadway. The reverend feeds him and gives him a job painting fences around the church and rectory with a bunch of other homeless boys. For Peter, it is perfect: without education or legs that function properly, his hands are his only tools for employment. Barney Gook helps him to apply for an invalid pension, gets him into intensive rehabilitation, where he begins training in a trade. Then the real prize, the key to Aladdin's cave – a driver's licence – that helps to bring him a job as an apprentice welder. Peter feels life is beginning all over again.

Sharon is so like her mother at sixteen: knowing but naive, confident but gullible. Unaware of how easy it is to lose all your hope and potential, for bad to disguise itself as good. So every boy who comes near her might as well be Michael: Yvonne questions and queries each one, his family, his job, his age, her eyes flicking over his clothes, his shoes, his hair. If he's good-looking she is anxious and scornful. What she wants are signs of decency.

But what to do, how to manage this feeling – a cauldron where her stomach should be – as she watches Sharon walk through the world now. She'd begun her warnings a year or so before: the dangers of boys. What you say and don't say, do and don't do, where you go and don't go. But now it's more urgent: the tomboy girl has turned into a swan. Dark-haired, shapely, legs like her mother's in sling-backs and her chin up to the world. She's already told her what happens to girls left alone with boys, in cars or houses or even at the beach. Now, she feels, she must speak plainly: *Greek men*, she warns. *They think Australian girls are easy. Sow their wild oats and then go off and marry a good Greek girl.*

This is what Yvonne doesn't know: Sharon is already sneaking into the dark and seedy nightclubs of Fortitude Valley, a fast fifteen-minute walk from home. It's deeply risky, Sharon knows; she'll be grounded if her mother finds out. But it's a compulsion: she's trying to find someone who looks like her. Since Andrew's birth, the face in the baby photo in her mother's room has returned to haunt her dreams. She adores Andrew, his easy baby smiles, his marble-dark eyes. She pounces on him in the mornings and after work, scoops him from his crib, singing as she goes about the house. She thinks of the hidden photo as she kisses Andrew's face, every time she coos and rocks him to sleep. Peter, Peter, Peter.

She is looking for her brother, she is looking for herself. There are many olive-skinned, dark-haired men in these cosmopolitan clubs, and she is young and good-looking, crystal-eyed. They ask her to dance, and as she moves around the floor with them she tries to find something in their voices, in their looks, in the things they say, that might tell her who she is. But excitement soon begins to feel like menace. It's their eyes.

One night she feels eyes across the room that make her perspire, make her feel like she hasn't washed. She feels fear lock into her belly, not for her own safety so much as this: what if Peter is among these men whose eyes make her something she's not? Is Peter like her or like them?

The words of her mother and grandmother beat in her head: *wild oats/womaniser/beat her black and blue*. She leaves the nightclub, wipes the lipstick from her mouth, flattens her teased hair and runs for the safety of the tram.

Seventeen, eighteen. Yvonne is by turns relieved and alarmed to learn that Sharon is going steady. He's a nice enough boy, not too good-looking. Easygoing, third-generation Australian, sandy featured, firmly Anglo-Celtic. But as the relationship deepens, there's a new anxiety, and the rules harden – she's not to sit outside with John in his Mini after a date, she's to come straight in. And midnight means midnight, not ten past. She's to avoid any situation – baby-sitting, for instance – where she and John are alone for hours. There are renewed warnings against 'heavy petting': *They'll say, if you loved me you would*, she tells Sharon, *but you can say: if you loved me you wouldn't*. Sex meant you had no self-control, the boy would see you as a *good time Charlie* and never respect you again, or you'd end up alone with a child – *and that's never easy, my girl*.

After one such warning Sharon surprises her with a confession. *I'm afraid I'll give in*, she says. Another lecture on self-control. But the next day when John breezes into the kitchen she takes them both to the bedroom her daughters share; seats John on one twin bed and joins Sharon on the other. Then: *Do you believe in sex before marriage for your sister, John?* She watches the lad's complexion change from sandy to scarlet, his desperate reach for words. *No, of course not*, he stammers out finally, keeping his eyes off Sharon.

Good, she says. *And I don't believe in it for my daughter. So keep your hands to yourself.*

Six weeks later they return to her. *We want to get married*, Sharon says. Eighteen is too young, she tells her, but John argues he is twenty-one and quite mature, he has a job and a car and prospects. Eighteen is too young, she repeats, until Sharon cuts in: *If we don't get married soon I'll get pregnant*, and she stops.

There is, she sees, no arguing now. The conversation finishes with, *If that's really what you want to do*. And only Sharon will know it isn't. That the whole idea is a relief and a shelter and an escape.

Sharon marries John eight weeks before her nineteenth birthday in the church where, just fourteen years before, Yvonne had married Arne. It is 1969. Elsewhere in the world, sexual freedom and women's liberation might be changing the way people perceive marriage, relationships and sex; but when Sharon steps down the aisle of St Paul's Presbyterian church on her father's arm, her face veiled and her dress of white guipure lace hugging a waspish waist, her mother's pride and relief are palpable. She beams. She has got this daughter safely to her wedding day, without mishap or scandal. Lightning has not struck twice.

She has made sure of it. Has sworn her daughters would be protected, as she had not been. That's how she saw it: that Veronica had failed her. She'd wanted her mother to *fight* for her. To protect her from bad men, insist she stay home and not go away with a man. This is what she tells us when we are in our teens: that we will be fought for, will be physically restrained if need be, if the situation demands it. If we want to go away with a boy, a man. If we look like making a mistake like that.

But we did make mistakes like that, and we did go away, my sister and I. Not at seventeen, but not much older. At the time, neither of us could recognise history tapping on our backs as we fell into young, even reckless, marriages, and I'd say neither of us would have heeded if we did. Our mother's vigilance throughout our adolescence – her tight scrutiny of our outings, the strict midnight curfews, her aversion to, almost prohibition of, any of us moving out to flat with friends – might have meant that, unconsciously, we began to regard marriage as a legitimate way to leave home. I wonder if, as we walked down the aisle at nineteen, both with several serious boyfriends behind us, our nervous mother was glad of it. If she was, her motives differed wildly from ours.

Just six years after Sharon walked down the aisle of St Paul's on our father's arm, I followed suit. Despite plans to travel and to write, I followed my heart to a small town just south of Cairns. I couldn't see that I was also following my mother: it felt like running away. But of course it was the same geography, the same stage, the backdrop of green cane fields, mountains, rain-soaked sky. The smell of the mills, bagasse burning, the sickly sweetness.

I couldn't see then – how could I? – the groove in the path already made, the tracks left by my mother. I jumped into a car with my new husband the day after our wedding and drove north into the teeth of my mother's history.

Lennart walks into our lives one ordinary day when I am fourteen. His physical presence is startling: he is a tall, blond seaman, with aquamarine eyes and a soft, easy manner. His merchant ship has just berthed at Hamilton Wharf.

Our father explains briefly: Lennart is his son from an earlier marriage, he says, just before Lennart arrives. We know nothing of him, or of his life on the other side of the world. We know nothing of our father's earlier life, or that it was sealed off by a promise our parents made to each other, long before we were born. We don't know about the letters Dad and Lennart exchanged, the late-night calls, the plans hatched and abandoned to bring him to Australia as a child. School, the language barrier, fear – all had prevented it. So this new information, the details, the history, can't feel real to a fourteen-year-old, not like the flesh-and-blood man here in our kitchen, an exotic bird blown in from the sea.

So even as Lennart walks through the door, shakes hands, and sits down at the table to drink coffee with Dad, my teenaged heart takes over. He's so handsome. So grown-up. So big-brotherly: he bends to talk to me in that familiar accent, he ruffles my hair. Calls me by my full name: Kristina. I swoon. The knowledge that we're siblings is too new, I can't absorb it and I can't calculate this supposed earlier life of our father at all. The facts feel faulty. I stare and stare at him, searching for clues, for connection, some verification of my father's words.

He takes us all down to his ship, where we scramble around decks and narrow passageways while he and Dad drink a toast to reunion in duty-free akvavit. But back at home, all of us around the red Laminex table, I'm mute. The others shyly answer his questions and ask their own, about Sweden, about life at sea. I lower my eyes if he looks in my direction, blush fiercely if he says my name. Just before I fall head over heels, he leaves. I watch him farewell our father, a lingering embrace, the soft sound of the word *Far*, and I remember. He's my brother.

Peter has gradually learned the rewards of work. There is a satisfaction in the exchange of labour and pay that he hasn't felt in his life on the streets, in the casual thieving, even in the shillings he's earned from Michael. And here's the surprising thing, unexpected: there is more money in honest jobs, he discovers, than in petty theft. Welding, taxi-driving, chauffering, carpentry. And they all deliver something to him besides cash – validation. A skill, a way of relating, and different ways of seeing the world.

But despite all this, he remains attached to risk, to the underside of things. That's where he's lived all his life: in a world just beneath the surface of safe. He's not entirely comfortable in the regular world, the world of confident, able bodies and unbendable rules. Life has made sure of that. There are many things he can't un-know.

So when he is asked to help renovate an old terrace in Surry Hills, to turn it into a brothel, he knows he has all the right aptitudes. He's not fazed by the owner's plans for *The Touch of Class*, and admires his ambition: to create an upmarket bordello, a themed fantasyland. There is nothing sordid in the notion. At the heart of it he sees a basic equation: the exchange of labour and reward. Just like any other job or business. As the project progresses he moves from carpentry to design, helping to conceptualise and assemble the various rooms: the *Chinese*, the *Garden*, the *Peacock*, the *Colonial*, the *Starlight*, the *Arabian*, the *Egyptian Spa*. He feels a surge of long-neglected creativity.

Everyone involved in *The Touch* is familiar: people on the margins, those who are, like him, happier away from the straight life and looking for some elusive sense of self. It restores his love of the edgy, of the blur of legal/illegal, the exotic. Though the risk, in the end, is low: all the right payments are made and dues paid to the right people. And the girls are well looked after, their health is scrupulously monitored, their pay is handsome, they are encouraged to extend their education, buy a house. Peter's pay packet is handsome too, even in his job as handyman and offsider, doing minor repairs, maintaining spas, delivering the pay-offs, deputising for the boss. He begins to feel what he's always suspected: that money removes barriers, lifts you, protects you. Gives you a whole new slant on who you are.

The bleak beacon of Peter's birthday, December 18, never wanes. It is booby-trapped. Mined with all her uncertainties, her grief. Year after year she steps warily towards it, watches its approach as she might a cloaked figure on an empty road. Beneath the cloak is the boy he once was and the man he might be now, the possibilities. Every singular fear she has walked with and slept with, nightmare and dream. But each year when the day arrives it is just that, a day that reeks of sadness. Nothing can remove that, not the spiced air of Christmas, the pudding in the steamer and the cake, the tinsel, not her other children pressing to be heard.

December 18, 1969 is more loaded than ever. She is a woman who likes to mark milestones, to commemorate, and Peter's twenty-first birthday is an occasion: the end of childhood, growing up. Freedoms and responsibilities, the key to the door. As with each of his birthdays she allows herself, briefly, to imagine his face. The shape of his thoughts and his eyes and his expectations. His joys and sadnesses. Does he wake on his birthday and think of her? The notion is consoling and terrifying at the same time. So she replaces it immediately – he is a man now, raised in the Greek way by a Greek family, and this day is theirs.

This is what she thinks as the birthday comes and goes, her head overruling her heart, protective. Except.

There is a word floating in and out of her consciousness, as it surely does for other mothers of sons now, at the end of the sixties and into the early seventies. *Vietnam*. As the protests simmer and explode on Brisbane streets and the carnage grows and the debate rages about a war we have no right to be in, she keeps to herself a terrible knowledge. She has a son of conscriptable age.

She reads the reports in the papers, looks at the pictures of marbles popping out numbers and fates, the faces of young men with fresh crew cuts, all trying to look pleased. Has he been called up? In which city or town? She scans the photos, reads the stories. The horrors of that war unfold and the death toll rises, and this is what she feels: the terrible irony of losing him not once but twice. The possibility.

For years Yvonne has wanted an ordinary house in the suburbs, and a proper garden, just like her younger siblings. She wants a life that matches theirs. Not a maze of old rooms behind a shop but a normal-looking house – brick, easy to clean – with roses and daisies and some herbs out the back. Nothing ostentatious, she hates that. Just the reassurance of streets that echo nothing back at you, not the past or your own ties to it. Ordinariness is what she craves. This is what she tells Arne when he decides to sell his business and they are released, at last, from its demands.

The house in Annerley, on the south side of the river, isn't exactly what she wants – the kitchen gets the late western sun and is stifling in summer, the bathroom is poky and she's tired of old tongue-and-groove boards that trap the dust. But there is something venerable in its lines, its lovely bay window, the crepe myrtle that splays against the white-painted walls in summer. There are roses in the front garden and a small lawn at the back, and it's close to schools and to Stone's Corner, where Ronnie's grandparents had been the first white settlers.

She is quietly proud of this family history, commemorated now in the name of a hotel and a suburb. James Stone had made roads and ginger beer for a living while he waited for a licence to run a hotel. In the meantime his wife, Mary Ann, produced eleven children in pioneer conditions; Old Gran, Eliza, was the ninth. Yvonne liked to remember that, though Stone's Corner was now an inner-city suburb, it was just 140 years since Mary Ann put her children to bed amid the utter blackness of thick bushland, and to the frequent near sounds of corroboree.

The Stones' place in history was important to Ronnie's wider family too. They clung to it, perhaps, as evidence of pioneer blood, of ambitious beginnings, a counterweight to the reduced straights in which some of them found themselves. As children, Yvonne and her siblings heard the stories of the slab hut, the ginger beer made in lieu of liquor, but they especially loved the story of James Stone's funeral. They all recounted it over the years; they seemed to imagine they had been there, that these were their own memories: the eerie silence as the horse-drawn funeral carriage led a procession past the Corner and the hotel their great-grandfather never got to brew in, past the Moreton Bay fig he planted outside. The procession's solemn pause outside the hotel entrance, beneath the now tall tree, and then the splintering sound – portentous, sudden – as a branch crashed to earth in front of the hearse. An unearthly sign, they all understood, that his life and his passing had been noted by some greater power.

My mother loved this story; she told it often when we were young. Even then, bent to my homework in the kitchen as she sewed, I could hear she was reaching for something beyond narrative: not just the undeniable ties to family and place, but,

I see now, her own connection to courage and dignity and respectability. The evidence was before her, if not in Ronnie then in Eliza, the warm and gentle grandmother she adored. To my mother, Old Gran was everything her own mother wasn't. She was civilised, measured, soft. As my mother's fingers guided fabric through the Singer, her voice another thread in the tack-tack of the needle, she was reassured by James Stone's and Eliza's lives: dignity and respectability might yet be innate, might be inherited, might be – despite mistakes and mischance – retrievable.

A new house, imperfect but in sight of this history, would do. She takes a job in the sewing room of the local hospital, a fifteen-minute walk away. Arne reminds her she doesn't need to work, but it's an old habit now: she vowed so long ago never to rely on a man for money again. Andrew is enrolled at a nearby primary school; she's there to collect him every afternoon at three o'clock, and together they walk home.

When Peter meets Kim he is flying a kite. As a metaphor it's too obvious. But it's true: there he is at the park, mucking around with friends, when she strolls up to join them. He's struck by her immediately, wants to impress her. It's a fairly low-key way to meet a woman; the kite, hooked by the wind, tugs upwards, the string creasing his palm.

She is looking for a job. *I know someone who wants a receptionist*, Peter offers, smiling. Well, she's a good-looking girl; he barely knows he's flirting. When he tells her the employer is *The Touch of Class* she doesn't blink.

It is the mid-seventies: the bordello is flourishing and the earnings from it, they think, are almost unseemly. In time, Peter and Kim become the owner's trusted deputies: Kim managing the office and Peter ensuring everything works, from the busy laundry to the spas. It's a business like any other, apart from its illegalities, its glancing acquaintance with the underworld. And after hours the whole world is theirs, or so it seems.

It's the high life – or the low life, depending on your perspective. On the proceeds of *The Touch* they travel, they wine and dine, they frolic on Sydney Harbour, on the glittering beaches of the Gold Coast. They drive expensive cars and wear expensive clothes. Peter tastes accomplishment for the first time, and affluence, and self-esteem. His real life rushes up to meet him.

Happiness, he is finding out, expands you. Opens up the chambers of your heart, so that the feelings you've choked – forgiveness, acceptance, the happiness of others – begin to live again, to breathe. *You are the world to me,* he says to Kim, trying to express what he feels. She says: *Love. Tell me you love me.* But the word, foreign to his tongue, won't come.

Still, his work at *The Touch* and his relationship with Kim have given him a confidence he's never felt before, and it makes him generous. For the first time he can look at his father and see something more than anger and cruelty. Can identify the times when Michael had shown patience and restraint, the times he *didn't* belt him, when he'd tried in his own way to reach out. Remembers the piano accordion lessons, his father on violin, teaching him notes. The rabbiting. The milkshakes offered to friends. It isn't much but it validates his impulse to visit him, validates a feeling of connection, despite all that's gone between them, all he's endured.

When Michael takes Sophia and young George to Kythera for three months and isn't back eighteen months later, Peter decides to go to him. With passport and ticket and plenty of spending money he flies to Athens. Books a passage on a ferry from Piraeus to Kythera. Kim will come too, a week later.

He arrives by boat and is immersed immediately in family. Surprised by welcome. Even his stepmother seems happy to see him, and Michael smiles widely as he introduces cousins, uncles, aunts. They gather round and shake his hand, hug him, nod and laugh. There are days and nights of dancing and backgammon, chess, swimming, talk. He absorbs it all like a sponge. Writes in his diary: *Nice that my father is so proud to show me off.* He notes the donkeys, the horse-drawn ploughs, the luxury of electricity at the beach. The water drawn from wells.

At a party in the village square, he watches his father dance. His body is lithe and strong even now: he leads the other dancers in the weaving line of the *Tsamiko* and the *Syrtos*, his body twisting through the steps. As the dance intensifies he leaps, clicks his heels, shouts. He is by far the best dancer here.

From his chair near the band, Peter sees the admiration of others. As the night progresses through its rounds of souvlaki, retsina and dancing he feels a mix of pride and envy: how he'd love to be able to dance with Kim. With any pretty girl. He'd love to be as good as his father, better than his father. He wants, in some way, to match him. To prove that he can.

But the following morning all that disappears in the warm Mediterranean. He swims out from the beach at Agia Pelagia, in the transparent blue, swims until the taverna is barely visible and he stops and floats, buoyed by salt. This is his element: in the water he is equal, to his father, to everyone. Here, in the embrace of the sea that gave birth to Aphrodite, he surrenders, and lets himself fall in love with Greece.

Kim gives birth to their daughter in 1983, and the baby, dark-haired and dazed at the suddenness of her Caesarean birth, is handed to her father. Peter looks into her eyes and finds them familiar, and the words come then, pushing out and dislodging a rush of emotion, as if it is he and not Kim who has been in long labour. He thinks: *I love you*. The once empty phrase now brimming with meaning. The child who wasn't loved, who was never told he was loved, is now a man poised on the brink of revelation. His head is tipped forward over his daughter, he might be weeping or he might be praying, and he sees his own eyes reflected back in hers. *Love*. It's as if *he* has just been born.

Mother love. Father love. In the weeks after Tamara's birth, there is an odd fusing in Peter's blood. Kim is ill in hospital, so it is he who drives across town to another hospital to feed the baby, to change her nappies, to coo and talk to her. They get to know the shape and sound of each other, father and daughter, as Peter walks his baby up and down corridors and into the gentle winter sunshine. As Tamara's eyes swivel and focus on the world, Peter begins to see new shadows of his own: his mother's and his, the eternal circle of arms cradling. Flesh of my flesh.

Less than two years later, Tamara is a copy of the sturdy, almond-eyed toddler that he was when his mother lost him. *The Touch* has been sold, along with their house. With money in their pockets, Peter and Kim cast about for a new life. They're thinking a motel, on the coast somewhere, a fresh start. Neither of them says anything when, driving out of Sydney, Peter turns the car north.

Peter and Kim drive up the Pacific Highway, with Tamara in the back and a caravan behind them. They're looking for real estate, the right business. But Peter's heart has business of its own. They can't agree on anything south of the Queensland border. By the time they reach the Bribie Island turn-off, an hour north of Brisbane, it's clear to Kim that Peter is driving, blindly or not, to Cairns.

They've already come more than a thousand miles with a cranky baby in a hot car; she won't go another thousand, not for anything. She wants to go back to Sydney. They argue and turn the car south once more, but as Brisbane looms up in their windscreen again, she softens, knowing what's in his head. *There'll be a registry in Brisbane*, she says, *births, deaths and marriages. Electoral rolls. Why don't we have a look?*

Years earlier he'd told her about the search for his mother. The blind running, questioning strangers, police, anyone. She'd looked at him, not quite believing. Then: *Jesus*, she'd laughed, *that's not the way you do it. Haven't you ever heard of official records?*

So here they are in the old sandstone building in George

Street, and Kim is suddenly sure that this is it: this time, they'll find her. It isn't exactly what she'd planned for the trip but now that they're here she's made the decision: they'll find her.

Now Peter is hurrying away from the inquiry counter waving the full copy of his birth certificate in the air: he's only ever had an extract, and it hasn't told him much. But this one has more names – those of Ernest and Veronica Ball – and these, she knows, are the clues they need.

They sit for hours, poring over telephone books and electoral rolls, as the baby sleeps and wakes and her cries echo up and off the beautiful high vaulted ceilings above them. Until Kim finds two sets of initials, *E* and *V*, that match up with the surname on the birth certificate, and she cries out too. *I think we've found your grandparents*, she says.

They drive to the address in Mt Gravatt listed in the electoral roll. An elderly woman in thick glasses opens the door, and Peter tells her he's looking for Yvonne Ball. She looks him up and down, says, *Who are you?* He tells her who he is. Ronnie's face betrays nothing. She's expressionless. But something has registered because it takes her several moments to respond.

Then she says in her unschooled vowels: *Oh, you're Mick's son. She won't want to see* you. There's not an ounce of softness or regret.

But then she tells him to hang on; doesn't ask him in, leaves him there on the landing at the top of the stairs while she shuffles away. Then she's back and thrusting a piece of paper at him, an address scrawled in a shaky hand. He takes it and thanks her and leaves.

It's a fifteen-minute drive from Mt Gravatt to Annerley, but it might be five or it might be fifty – they don't notice. The car is a self-contained vessel, powered by emotion; Kim watches the play of anxiety and fear and excitement across Peter's face. A sentence keeps playing in her head: *We're going to see his mother.* She talks quietly to him, tries to calm him down, but she's secretly anxious too, worried that it will all explode in front of them. She wonders what kind of picture they present, she and Peter and Tamara, and unconsciously she turns to the baby and checks she's tidy. As she looks at her own child, another thought comes, something unexpected: how will *she* cope, this mythical mother, this long-imagined woman in Peter's head? Kim's a bit worried about her too.

They find the house, a white-painted Queenslander with bay windows and roses at the front, and park across the road. Before Kim can utter a word, Peter is out of the car.

He pushes open a gate between rose bushes and walks up the front stairs. Nausea growls in her stomach as she watches him. He is a boy once more, standing there; he might as well be holding his heart, torn from his chest, as the piece of paper that is still in his hands. But there's no one home. He limps back and slides into his seat. They sit in the car and wait.

They look around them. By Sydney standards it's an inner-city street, but there's a suburban feel in its gardens and in the relative quiet. The house is similar to its neighbours: high-set and well tended, perhaps thirty or forty years old. An ordinary enough house, nothing to distinguish it, to set it or its occupants apart. Still, it tells them something of the people who live here: they're not rich and they're not poor. Well, not outwardly. The roses and the crisp white paint give it a homely feel, Kim thinks. It's cared for.

With their quick nervous eyes they follow the steps of every woman who passes. Tamara has dropped off to sleep in the back. Kim is surprised – there's so much adrenalin pumping around the car, she was sure the baby could feel it. And now there's another woman on the footpath, and their eyes don't miss a thing, not her energetic walk, her dark hair, the shopping she carries. They watch this woman – she seems the right age, that's all they can tell – and for some reason they stop talking. As if words, sounds, might impede their vision, one sense diminishing the other. It seems important to be quiet. So they're silent, their faces turned to the woman as she reaches the house. Stops. Turns into the gate near the roses. The roses, the roses. *Oh my God*, Peter breathes. *That's my mother.*

She has walked home from work at the hospital today via the supermarket. Sometimes she'll find one of her children waiting outside the laundry to drive her, a nice surprise but she never expects it, rouses on them for taking time out of their day. It's only a fifteen-minute walk and pleasant in winter, though in summer she sweats freely, mopping her face, hating the heat.

She's carrying a few groceries and doesn't stop at the mailbox or among the flowers in the front garden, but walks straight past them and down the side path to the back steps. She doesn't seem to notice the car and caravan parked across the street, or the faces turned towards her. Well, it's a busy street in an inner-city suburb; there are always cars. She wants to move, when the youngest is finished school and university, to a quieter place and a low-set house. A couple of years earlier she fell down these steps as dawn broke on her way to work, needed surgery on a shattered ankle. It was the first bone she'd ever broken. She was proud of that.

In the kitchen she pushes open windows and fills the kettle. She is spooning coffee into a mug when she hears the knock at the back door.

She opens it to a good-looking, dark-haired man. Perhaps he's somewhere in his thirties, it's hard to tell. But her body feels a bolt of recognition; something opens inside her, then slams shut. It's what she's taught herself to do.

He says, *I'm looking for Yvonne Ball.* Her maiden name. She feels invisible fingers claw open a possibility. The man – for some reason she thinks *boy* – tilts his head and smiles. *You don't recognise me,* he says.

The possibility.

Her heart, trained well by now, lurches. She puts her hand to it, admonishing. Casts around for any other name, mutters one, not his.

But the man on the step doesn't seem to hear. He's still smiling. Then: *I'm Peter,* he says, two words to stop the world. *I'm Peter, your son.*

She stands at the door and struggles to stay upright, to remain in that moment, looking at the face she's sought so long. Lifts her hands towards him. Then notices the woman, behind Peter and several steps below.

The woman is smiling too, holding a baby. A girl, brown as a nut, dark-eyed. It is, she knows immediately, her granddaughter.

Would you like to come in? she says then, trying to control herself, her voice, her heart, her hands. What to do, what to say, how to be? *Would you like some coffee?*

She stands back. Peter steps over the threshold.

And there it is, cruel and sudden: the thirty-six years without her is manifest, tangible, in his limp, in his heavy, built-up shoe.

Peter stands before his mother. The words in the air between them — *I'm Peter, your son* — and they might be a gauntlet thrown as well as an introduction. He's anticipated rejection; that's who he is, that's what he knows. But the seconds tick a new man into being: some light has switched on in his mother's eyes and her face, her whole body leans towards him. She opens her arms.

Later, he will say there are no words for his feelings in that instant. Only one thing is approximate: his first glance of his newborn child the year before.

She says she needs to do something with her hands. They're shaking. So she re-fills the kettle and goes to the telephone. Three calls. They hear her say it three times — *There's someone I want you to meet.* The words, and the woman, enigmatic. Back in the kitchen she pours coffee, takes patty cakes from a tin, carries them to the dining room. Bends and lightly touches the baby's head. Is she hungry? What does she need? And to Peter: *Your father warned me. I was never to come near you.*

But Peter is barely registering the words. At that moment they are almost superfluous to the way she looks at him, her voice when she speaks. He is not a demonstrative man but he finds himself thinking of the embrace they shared at the door, his arms folding around her in some muscle memory of the last time, those years before. He watches her and listens to her and wants to feel that embrace again.

Kim watches too, trying to contain her daughter, and her own emotions. This warm woman, this mother, Peter's face turned up to her like a boy's. She'd been almost undone by the sight of them in the doorway earlier, their eyes so alike and wet with tears. Now she sits at the table in this reassuringly ordinary house and is surprised by tears again: the brothers and sisters coming in the door, saying Peter's name. They cry and laugh and hug him, hug their mother. She can only think of their great good luck: this nice, average family, the love ricocheting between them.

And then Arne. He comes in the door and Kim sees a slender man in khakis, tanned, bespectacled. She's watching his mouth, hoping for generosity. He smiles, and she barely notices how Yvonne introduces them because she's watching and listening as Arne says *Welcome* and grasps Peter's hand and shoulder. *I'm very glad to meet you*, he says and it's accented and oddly formal but she hears that he means it. *You are welcome here.*

The room grows loud with talk and preparations for dinner. Kim registers the particular attention Yvonne pays her, making sure she is not lost in the family's exuberance, that Tamara isn't overwhelmed. Tamara's grandmother. She feels a fledgling hope that the circle might have turned. Peter has found his mother, he is no longer lost. He has been lost the whole time she has known him, still the six-year-old boy on the train from Dungog, asking strangers if they'd seen his mother, the teenager hitching to Cairns to find his mother, to find himself. She feels a welling gratitude to this family, but especially to this woman. Now that Peter knows he has a warm and decent mother, he may be able to concede the warmth and decency in himself. His potential for love. Now, she thinks, everything might change.

Later she will ask him and Peter will tell her: *I can't believe it. I didn't expect it, the acceptance. The emotion.* And she understands that he is overwhelmed by inclusion, by everything he sees he has missed.

She spreads a white cloth over the extended table and sets out her best china. She's always loved Mikasa, its plain elegance, white plates rimmed in silver. Spare chairs are found and dusted, vegetables are peeled and roasted and steamed. Arne is despatched to buy wine – *What kind?* she asks someone, and to her husband, *Something nice.* She counts out cutlery, the magic of the numbers, an extra three – *three* – and listens to the sound of shy conversation from the lounge room, the young ones playing. Tries to fight outrage: his leg, his pain, everything she's missed. And hardest: the father's face in the son's.

In the bathroom now she pulls a comb through her wavy hair. Regrets not colouring it the week before. Regrets – but only momentarily – the surprise of it; she might have put on some makeup, earrings, a better dress. Still. She is what she is, a middle-aged woman. She leans into the mirror, trying to see what he sees. Smooths eyebrows with a fingertip, finds her lipstick. Steadies herself. As if, after all, this is an interview for a job she dearly wants. Then, reassured by the talk rocking back and forth in the next room, she slips away from them all, down the front steps to the garden.

The night is cool and clear, at once ordinary and utterly transformed. She stands alone among her flower beds, breathing. Is startled, when she lifts her eyes, by the car and caravan, unfamiliar in yellow street light; they might belong to strangers. Her *son*. All the things he might have been told, all the things he doesn't know. Thirty-six years of longing have funnelled down to this evening, in this week, in this life. She can hardly bear it. Can feel her own heartbeat in her wrists, behind her eyes.

She turns back to the garden. There it is in front of her, one unlikely, perfect rose. They'll never believe it when she tells them its name – a Blue Moon, long-stemmed, singular. She leans into the face of the flower, its skin-like petals. Her fingers tremble on the secateurs. Then she gathers herself, parts the surrounding stems and makes a clean diagonal slice. A wayward thorn traces a fine line across her thumb, but she barely feels it; turns and retraces her steps to the stairs. In the dining room she puts the rose in a slender vase in the middle of the table and calls them all to dinner.

Sharon and Peter exchange looks across the room. Their mother wonders if they see what she sees: not just resemblance but equivalence, one shape locking into the other. Kinship, and their mother's eyes. That much is clear, and safe, unlike the phantom shape of a father between them. And as for allegiances: she knows these might show themselves only in the tentative days to come, when questions will be cautiously asked and answers as cautiously given. When they begin the long process of assembling their separate pasts, the search for points of recognition.

For now, here on her lap those separate pasts evaporate: Tamara. She feels the baby's skin against her own, and a transfusion of love and longing. She murmurs to her, coaxing her to eat while her own food cools on the plate, and as she does Tamara looks up and into her grandmother's eyes. She sees Peter watching, his knife and fork lowered, and smiles as an empress smiles.

Talk rises and falls around the table. She sits at its centre, an ordinary woman with an ordinary husband and children, in her ordinary house. This is what she wants him to see: the decency of it. There is nothing fancy about her life, nothing showy, but neither is there anything drab. All around is the evidence of a humble life, she thinks, a good life but a hard-working one, a deserving one. With this thought she looks around to check, suddenly seeing everything through his eyes. The tongue-and-groove walls, the Laminex kitchen with its stove recess and original cupboards. She doesn't much like the vinyl of the lounge room furniture. She likes the authentic and the old, the roll-top desk she bought her husband for his fiftieth birthday, the curtains and candlesticks and picture frames from Arne's mother's house in Sweden. The upright brass ashtrays she'd found in antique shops, the landscapes painted by her father and brothers.

But when Tamara finally wriggles from her knee she knows she can't guess how her son sees all this, not yet. Can't guess his opinion. She has no idea what to calibrate it by; no idea of his attitudes and tastes and the houses he has lived in, his view of what is true and what is fake, what is real and what is false. The type of woman he sees when he looks at her, the woman he has for a mother.

When her daughters begin to clear the table she finds herself alone with her son. All the fear and apprehension, the questions unasked. And the conversation she knows she can't begin, not now, because it has no discernable end. It might last another thirty-six years. So instead, she reaches over and touches her palm to his face. And can't help herself: she says, *If I'd thought for a moment you'd want to see me. Your father* – and Peter stops her, he says, *It's all right, Mum, I know the old man, I've been running away from him since I was six*. She wipes tears with the heel of her hand, and then her gaze drops to his leg, to his built-up shoe – a boot really, it reminds her of something out of Dickens. She says: *That must have been hard for you, Peter.* And Peter shrugs in the way she'll soon come to recognise. *There are people with worse*, he says. He looks into her eyes then. *I don't let it stop me.* She hears both reassurance and a statement – he is whole, just like these others. And that is what she will say to Evelyn when she calls the next day: *He's done carpentry, he's done welding, he says 'I don't let it stop me'.* And Evelyn will hear the pride in her sister's voice, and her heart will break a little. Everything her sister has lost.

She lies in darkness beside her sleeping husband. But there will be little sleep for her tonight. Shock still pumps through her body; she is here and not here, caught in a bizarre world that has her watching herself from above. Watching this man, her son. She has spent so many years dreaming of this day, wanting it and fearing it in equal measure. In the next few days, as she sits over endless coffee with him, driving, talking, measuring each word, she will feel the sting of both, the desire and the fear, as she counts the cost of all the years lost. And as Peter prepares to return to Sydney, the potential of a whole new kind of grief.

As for the rest of us: in the weeks that followed we told ourselves a story, a fiction about a boy lost and found, a family reunited, a mother's grief dissolved. It was simple: Peter was back; we'd get on with the business of including him in our lives. There in front of us was the happy ending we'd always strived for, unknowingly, for our mother. We had only to enact it every day.

But it wasn't simple and it wasn't a story. It wasn't entirely happy and it wasn't even an ending. Peter embodied the fracture at the centre of our lives, and though we didn't yet know why, I think we suspected it. How else to explain the way we allowed the months to close over his sudden appearance, like water over a sinking ship? We simply decided that, now Peter was back, everything would be all right. Perhaps because the stakes were so high: truth and deception, guilt and blame, loyalty, faith and trust. And most of all: our mother's happiness. We decided to believe that all the missing joy had been retrieved.

But we all learned, gradually, that some things can't be retrieved. Our mother would never get back her baby boy. Peter would never retrieve the childhood he should have had. Still, they tried. Everybody tried. In this story, everyone did the best they could with what they had.

Who is this person Peter is in his family's eyes? He's spent his whole life constructing himself as an outsider, someone who doesn't fit any of the shapes others do. There are so many things he hasn't figured out. Mostly: what a son is, what a brother is. But no one is telling him how it's done. He has no notion of how to behave. Nothing in his life has prepared him, not even his dreams. He realises that, all his life, he has only ever imagined having a real mother; he hasn't imagined being this mother's son. Being mothered: endless days in which love flows like milk, days he walks through as a prince does, as cherished as the moon but as ordinary. Just like every other boy he knows.

He wants to behave well, to be good enough. But she's been mythical, a fairytale, for so long that he is left with no real, flesh-and-blood way to respond. He has to make it up as he goes. In Brisbane he'd watched his brothers, looking for clues. He saw how easy they were with her, their arms flung casually over her shoulders, their thoughtless kisses. But their thoughtlessness is full of knowledge of her, the years of being her sons. He has only moments, hours to go on, to tell him what to do. For Peter, there can be no casual.

And in Brisbane, no one is telling her either, this mother newly made in a stranger's image. The runaway train of her past has come roaring towards her in the shape of her lost son, and without warning – though of course, like him, she has been preparing for this day since he disappeared. Now that he has found her, that's all she can see, those long years of not looking, the countless days he's had to wonder why she hasn't.

In the charged air left in the wake of Peter's departure, she goes about her ordinary days. She gets up early, packs lunches for her husband, her son and for herself, lays the breakfast table. She works eight hours in the hospital laundry's sewing room, mending sheets and uniforms, making small-talk in her coffee break, telling no one her news. Why would she? She has spent thirty-six years becoming this person, this blameless woman her workmates see every day. She doesn't want the younger version of Yvonne made vulnerable again.

Except. Alone at her sewing machine, or at home in her garden or kitchen and mostly in her dark sleepless bed, young Yvonne comes back and melds with the older one. She fears that neither is blameless; both have failed Peter. The younger one lost him but the older one ensured he stayed lost. This is what she believes, on and off. Forget the father's threats and her own assumptions. She could have saved him. He was sick and maimed and abused and isolated and she might have intervened. Might have found him. Instead this maimed and abused boy has found her. She has failed him twice.

★

She is the first to make the trip south to Sydney. She goes alone: this is, after all, not a holiday so much as a voyage of discovery. This is the journey she's always wanted to make: she's going to find her son. But it takes as much courage as it might have all those years before, a vulnerability she has layered over and numbed. This time, she's the one with her heart in her hands.

In the sitting room at the house in Lugarno, they begin. They bring their best versions of themselves to this work, their best intentions, their terrible need to make it all work. For Peter, this means looking ahead, not behind. He has his mother to himself for the first time in his life. His *mother*. He can't quite believe it. Wants to talk and drive her around and show her his life. He wants her to notice, to be impressed, to see him in his habitat and be proud. To see how well he has done, how accomplished he is, how *worth keeping*. How much he deserves to be her son.

So her apology takes him completely by surprise.

It seems to encompass his whole life: the failure of the marriage he was born into, the circumstances of his loss. Her absence. He'd never thought that was her fault, not consciously. But he hears her out, despite the tears she hurries to wipe away, that threaten to engulf them both. The pain in her eyes. He finds himself nodding, recognising his own. He says: *Mum, stop. You don't have to explain. I know what he's like.* He pauses. *I saw it with Sophia.*

But still. Things have to be said. *I'm sorry, Peter.* She looks at him steadily now. *I'm sorry for what you went through. If I'd thought for a moment . . . but your father warned me off, and the lawyers told me to leave you alone.*

She won't tell him the worst of her own life with Michael, the violence, the abuse, the starvation. The things Michael said as he wrenched Peter away. How can she tell him? Michael is his father, the only one Peter has known. She knows he still visits him, takes him to the races occasionally; hearing this makes her cautious. But the not telling costs her, as it always has. All the things Peter doesn't know.

She tries her best to fit in to their normal days, to cause no fuss, to help around the house and with the baby. To be, with Peter, the mother she's always been with the others – would always have been with him. She admires the house, the garden; tells Kim what a wonderful wife and mother she is. Plays with Tamara and croons to her, the way she has with each of her grandchildren. She tries hard to be herself. It is just what Peter wants: her attention.

One day she produces a small parcel: his first birthday present. An electric razor, a Braun. The brand is important – respected, high quality, but not ostentatious. She has agonised over the choice; it's like buying a gift for a stranger. What does he have, what would he like? Nothing too small, nothing too showy. But in the end, it's perfect: in its gestures to the personal, to the masculine, it says, You are a man, my son. Five years later, when things have changed, when nothing is working, the razor stops working too. It will take him another ten years to throw it out.

Do any of us understand our roles, daughter and son? Looking back, it's hardly surprising that, after thirty-six years and with a thousand miles between them, Peter struggles with that very notion daily, assuming he is the only one who does.

He's trying hard to be what he *thinks* a son should be. Courteous, courtly even. He finds he wants to bring her gifts, proof of all his abilities – to be a proper son, a proper husband and competent citizen of the world. Like a toddler, he wants to show her his devotion with shiny pieces of knowledge, bright pictures, small boasts, artefacts from a past he managed to get through without her: friendships, skills, decency, a bank account. It is an odd mix of barely conscious impulses: to prove to her he was all right all along, without her; to show her how clever and good he is and therefore how deserving of her; to keep her now that he has found her, so she'll never want to be without him again.

And partly, hidden deep, perhaps a desire to punish her too; no matter what anyone says – despite what his own head echoes – she wasn't there, she wasn't there. He needed her, she didn't find him, he missed out. He's seen what he missed out on now. The life he might have had. He wants to show them *all* that, despite her absence and theirs, he is okay. Better than okay. It's what he's taught himself to do.

So many slights and barbs, small and large, the myriad misunderstandings. They both hold up shields to protect themselves against pain, against another wrenching apart. They both feel the power the other has to hurt them, each gesture and action, one to the other, might mean something else, contain its opposite, contain its own worst outcome.

The nervous wonder, the conditional joy. Every wave of happiness has an undertow of fear. With every intuitive step towards him she loses a piece of her armour, the steeliness that has worked so well until now. Sometimes, she wants to snatch it up and reattach herself to safety. Whenever Peter speaks about his father she hears only the lies Michael has told, can see only the woman Peter must have had in his head all those years. A prostitute, cruel, heartless. A woman who cared so little for her baby son that she could abandon him. Who didn't just run away, but went off with *a German*. Her defensiveness re-ignites.

She can't get this particular slander out of her head. One morning, just after her return from Sydney, I dropped in to see her. She was in the laundry under the house; I asked her about her week away. But all she really wanted to talk about was Michael, the things Peter might yet believe. I watched her face as she bundled clothes around, angrily pushing sheets into the machine. *Why would he tell him that?* she said, seething. *That I'd run away with a German?*

At first I wondered why she couldn't see. *What are the worst things you could say about a woman,* I said, *in the decade after World War II?* But she wasn't really hearing and in the flash of her eyes I saw her question had been rhetorical. She was really asking me about the kind of a woman Peter had in his head. What kind of woman, what kind of mother? I was surprised by the voltage of her anguish then. Not any more. The unfairness of it, the injustice. And this: that after all these years, Michael was still capable of hurting her. He could still get at her through her son.

Is that how Peter saw it? He told her the stories, answered her questions, and whether he was conscious of it or not his words turned into weapons. Who could blame her if she felt it was intentional, the payback of an injured child? And who could blame Peter if he'd believed his father's lies, if even as a child he'd absorbed a fraction of them as truth? As an adult he believes it was the reverse: that with those stories he was trying to tell his mother something about Michael, not about her, about the kind of man he grew up with. *The old man was so vindictive,* he says. *His lies drove me towards her, not away.* But at the time she didn't see it that way. With every word and every story, she began to believe her son had found her to deliver the punishment she'd always believed she deserved.

These are the things that mother and son don't understand, or don't know how to manage: the shame of losing a child and the shame of being lost. The wariness and suspicion and terror in finding and being found. The moratorium on mourning they'd both endured since their separation, the unresolved grief that froze their hearts. They don't know, now the separation is over, how to lift that moratorium. They don't see that they are testing each other, as adolescents and parents do, needling each other for proof of their love and commitment, their fitness for the role of mother, of son. And that they need their whole lives, and the mercy of good counselling – rather than denial and the limited time they'll have – to recognise and name all this, to get past the bad abandoning mother and the damaged unlovable boy, to a place where both of them are blameless, both of them forgiven.

Neither can know the depths and complexities of the other's suffering. How can they – how can any of us – understand this: that before Peter's return, she had responded to his absence as might the mother of a missing person or soldier. He was neither here, alive, nor there, dead. There was no stencil for this kind of grief – no evidence of his life, no ceremony for his loss. No public mourning. For her own emotional survival, her response couldn't be partial. It was there in the conversation she had with my father before they married: the past was put away. Peter was gone; she had to face life without him.

So in the difficult years that followed the euphoria of his return, it was easy for her to slip back into those absolutes – and we, of course, from long habit, followed suit. We tried not to exacerbate her sadness by acting differently, so we dealt with Peter the way she did. If all was well between them, all was well between us all. But when it wasn't, when there was confusion and doubt and anger, when she slipped on her defensive armour and distanced him, so did we. We couldn't risk being distanced too.

When Sharon tells her she is going to see Peter, she feels a rock form in her belly. She can't help it; has never been able to shed the expectation that the worst is likely to happen. *You're going to see* him, *aren't you?* she says in response to the news, and watches her daughter's face. She has always been able to read her and to extract the truth in this way. Sharon may accuse her of *guilt induction* but that's just her fancy psychological training. She's merely demanding a spade be called a spade.

Sharon looks back at her and seconds tick by. She says finally: *Mum, I'm going to see Peter.* But the words are tumbling from Yvonne now, and louder: *You'll see Michael, you'll see Peter's father, he'll fill your head with stories. It's not fair on your father.*

Her daughter blinks. Purses her lips. *I think Dad understands that* he *is my father,* she says quietly. *And always will be.*

When Sharon does come face to face with Michael, she feels numb. There is no bolt of connection or recognition, no impulse to look into his eyes and see herself. She feels only a curiosity: so *you're* the man my mother fell for, those are the hands that hurt her. She almost says it: *you?* Because the man in front of her is old and small, his body and his power shrivelled. She feels something subside in her.

She had never consciously wanted this meeting, never dreamed or imagined it. On this first visit to Sydney Peter asks her and she is unequivocal: *No*. Perhaps it's her mother's and grandmother's words, or the Pandora's Box of emotion it might threaten to open up. But Peter has ideas of his own. He goes out for milk one day and brings Michael back.

There is a photograph of the meeting: the three of them, Michael, Sharon and Peter. They look relaxed enough for the camera – even Michael manages a half-smile, sitting next to the daughter he'd denied so long and still refused to claim. *She's not mine*, he said to Peter in Greek. What it might have cost him: the two faces in front of him are mirror-images, after all. *Your mother was very beautiful*, is all he will say in English, and when Sharon counters with *Then why did you hurt her?* he retreats behind a screen of language. Shrugs: I don't understand. It doesn't matter. On this day Sharon has the upper hand. She's leaped across an emotional chasm and met the man who fathered her, and she's confirmed her own truth. Her own power. *He was never part of me*, she says later, *he was always just Peter's father. He's never been mine.*

Yvonne would never have been able to say it, but despite the admiring glances she'd attracted in her youth, she's been ambivalent about her body since those terrible months in Cairns. The slaps and shoves and punches, the miscarriage – Michael's loathing of her flesh soon became her own. That younger Yvonne might look at the physical and psychic bruises and decide that, really, she herself is at fault. Weak and literally diminished by abuse, she might go on to think that the loss of her child was pre-scripted: she was already so much to blame. A good woman would have held on tighter. Her blood beating shame and deficiency to her heart every day.

So when her blood literally turns against her, when her cells turn on each other, the white lazily devouring the red, there is a part of her that isn't surprised. Leukemia, the doctor says, and that part of her receives it as her due.

Where does the pain of grief and loss live? In the head, in the heart, in the body? Who knows if anguish and illness are

230

linked, or the physical effects of a broken heart? For the rest of us the news means only shock and grief and terror. We don't notice the spectre of punishment that has haunted her since Peter's return. As the months go by, the years, with the reassurance that this form of the disease moves sluggishly, we hold on to that as if it's a safety rope, and we're dangling from a high cliff. As if the rope might save *us*. But the grieving has already begun. Each year, each year, each month holds within it a deadly potential; each birthday, each Christmas is charged with both joy and despair.

We do anything we think might save her, or at least ease her fears, or our own. Anything to keep her with us. I suppose we reverted to our childhood selves, trying, and often failing, to be good, or good enough. We would gather the family, cook her favourite food, sit with her through doctor's appointments and blood tests and treatments. Each of us, at some stage, discovers an exotic cure after long research. Or just turns up to drink tea or weed the garden or be fitted for the clothes she still loved to cut and sew, all the things that tell us that all is right with the world.

Part of us thinks we're succeeding. This, surely, is what is required. But we fail too. Disappoint her with our deficiencies, marriages that slip through our fingers, poor judgment, arguments, all of it evidence of our frailty, which she has always seen as her own.

At home in Sydney Peter hears the news from Sharon. He slumps in his chair. *I've just found her*, he thinks, *and now I'm going to lose her.* A second time. It's like a repeat, a re-enactment, and he feels as helpless as he might have been the first time. It would take several years – and the death of his father in

Sydney – for him to see there's one thing to do: return to Queensland. To prevent that second loss, to wrap his arms around her tighter. Fifty years before, he hadn't held on hard enough. But there'd be no wife and child with him; his impulse to move, this relentless pull to the north, is the line in the sand for his marriage. The man in him knows that, but the boy in him wins. He packs up his belongings and his child-like heart and drives towards his mother.

In Brisbane he rents a tiny flat and tries to reinvent himself. He sets up a small business with Andrew, and sets about inserting himself into the physical and emotional landscape of his family. He visits, turns up at family functions, tries out this new version of himself. Attempts to relinquish his solitary nature, his distrust of emotion. It is another hard thing in a long line of them. He struggles to keep his faith and optimism as his savings diminish and a new and needling pain pierces not just his leg but his whole body, arms, neck, back. Later he would hear the term *post polio* and recognise its mark, but at the time he dismisses the pain as self-pity. Ignoring it, however, doesn't send it away.

So when his income begins to shrivel and his mother offers him the spare bedroom in the new house she and Arne had built in the quiet outer suburbs, he feels torn between relief and terror. He has his mother's attention, but not on the terms he'd planned. He'd wanted to be in control of his life here, to prove he was successful and accomplished. Going home to live with his mother – even one he'd never lived with before, even one in the grip of serious illness – feels adolescent. Feels like failure.

When she comes across the lyrics to 'The Rose', she remembers Bette Midler's voice on the radio, one woman singing to another, and they speak to her immediately, about the past and the present. She'd always known about the strength required for love, the tensile quality of it, the intricate balance of loneliness and luck. Perhaps she has lost faith in her own ability to calibrate those scales; perhaps she sees these words as talisman, and slips them between cottons and lace in a dresser drawer. As her illness progresses she might feel the need for one. Or for a reminder of the tenacity of life, of the seeds that we plant. Tenacity was a quality she valued above all others. Her own would see her through a decade of chemotherapy and change: through the deaths first of Ernest, then of Veronica and one of her younger brothers; the divorces of daughters, the births of grandchildren, the weddings of her two younger sons. And the disappearance, for the second time, of her eldest. This time she tells herself she has done as much as she can to hold him – though uncertainty and anger coil in the corner of her days.

Still, when Andrew's daughter Ruth is born nearly ten weeks early, she cries for the precariousness of life. But celebrates her arrival nonetheless – even so tiny she is still beautiful, so obviously her granddaughter, and she spends whole afternoons with her hands thrust through the windows of Ruth's humidi-crib, touching her into strength. But she is anxious too and can't settle, not until Ruth comes home, until she can hold her. They are almost inseparable then, Yvonne and this new baby, this new outlet for her love, for her great capacity to do good, make better.

There is catastrophe in the air in 1999, as the year limps to an end. People worry over computers, avoid aircraft, store up supplies, nervous of impending cataclysm as the millennium turns. Then 2000 dawns and the clocks still tick, the sky holds fast, the stars, the sun. But for how much longer, we wonder, as our mother weakens. Surely the stars know, aloft in galaxies that look faded to us too, as if light is leaking from them.

Twelve years have lulled us into near-denial. She's fought like a leopard fights and won for so long. A small part of each of us refuses to see she is losing, we can't look. But another part is on alert. That heightened sense not only of mortality but of the world and all its likely portents, days too still, the shape of clouds, the movement of wind through leaves. Late night storms. Our mother, we know, was born in a storm.

We all have our ways of keeping her alive. When she's in hospital Ashley sits with her each morning, ticking off her hospital menu card with hearty, too-big meals she won't be able to eat. I take in a book to read aloud, page by page, breath by breath with her. Willing her to want to hear the story out.

Andrew takes Ruth, knowing how restorative her very presence is. And Dad, as he has all his life, takes her flowers. We'd admire them when we arrived; she would smile and say: *The boyfriend*.

Sharon flies up from Adelaide. If her mother is home from hospital they resume an old habit, and rise with the dawn to talk over tea. For Sharon these mornings become memories she stores in herself as a squirrel stores acorns against the winter. It's easy between them now. They talk softly and remember and laugh, careful not to wake Arne. It's just the two of them, and it reminds her of the days before there were more, when it was she and her mother walking the dark corridors at Clinton, or singing on the back steps at Cannon Hill. But she is also aware that her mother is doing a kind of reckoning: when she speaks of Peter there is an edge in her voice, bitterness one day, disappointment the next, as if she is hoping to be challenged, her mind changed, that Sharon will magically produce reasons to believe she is wrong. That Peter is not staying away to hurt her, or because he resents her, or because, at this stage of the long and painful game, he holds all the cards.

But Peter doesn't even know he's in the game. He knows only that his presence is some kind of irritant that his mother doesn't need now. He is torn between the shame of staying away as she weakens and his suspicion that it is his own weakness that keeps him here. He is afraid of her anger and longs for her approval. But he can't seem to be the person she wants him to be.

He reassures himself with his own pain: his leg, his arms, his back. One night he slips and falls on a rainy pavement in Newtown, and it feels like someone has taken a chainsaw to his right ankle. He tries to ignore it, limping each day to his new job in a computer store and at night, dousing the pain in his leg and his heart with whisky in his Newtown flat.

When the call comes, he succumbs to its devastation. *Like a bomb hit me* – the aptness of the phrase, he thinks, as he looks out at a world bleak and ravaged, more savage than he'd ever known it even as a lonely child. For days he almost enjoys the chainsaw at his ankle and lets himself cry – realising she has taught him, not by crying herself but by allowing it, making room. His brothers and sisters, he remembers, weep at the drop of a hat. He packs his bag for Brisbane.

Our mother died on an ordinary day unheralded by the signs or portents we'd looked for. No storm. There'd been no emergency call to the hospital. Later we'd note how extraordinary it was that, though Sharon was in Adelaide and Peter was in Sydney, so many of us were there that Sunday morning when her body finally overcame her will.

This is what we found hard to believe that day: that her body had simply stopped fighting. I think our own bodies refused it, momentarily, and then, as one, we turned to our father. Held him so he wouldn't fall. Watched him stroke her face and hair and call her *darling*. We held each other, we held our mother, cupped her face, held her hands and thanked her. Told her we loved her, cried for her and for ourselves. Trembled in the new and frightening world without her in it.

We called Sharon and Peter. We called Evelyn. And finally we went home with our father, to the house still so palpably hers, imprinted with her thoughts and conversation, her busy hands. We barely left it, then, until the funeral five days later. Sharon came, and Peter, and we were all caught in a net of safety we could feel only if we were together. We cancelled work. If we had to go out we hurried back again; the rest of the world felt too raw and uncaring, and grief was a stranger there. In our parents' house grief nurtured us that week, buffered us against the time to come. We ate and drank and talked together, we cried and we remembered, we made arrangements for pastor and chapel. We slept wherever we fell.

There were no differences between us then. How could there be? When we looked around the table we saw her in each other's face; with her death each one was more precious somehow, all part of her. And if Peter had been lost again we knew the reasons were as complex and unknowable as our mother, as Peter himself. We felt it all dissipate in this new and fragile air.

The day of the funeral was showery; Peter drove to the shop to buy spare umbrellas. We all fussed with our clothes, trying to decide. In the end I picked a pink dress Mum had made for me, and laughed out loud to see that everyone – all the women, at least – had thought the same way. All the things she'd sewed. Our father wore his suit; he asked Sharon to help with his tie, as he'd done all our lives. When she'd finished we looked around at each other, and at our children, all dressed up for their grandmother, and realised that then, as always, we wanted her approval. We climbed into the cars and clutched each other's hands as we drove away.

The funeral was both mourning and celebration. We tried to do what she had done: salvage something. From the horror of losing her, and so young, just sixty-nine, and from the past painful twelve years. We'd all contributed words to a eulogy, weighing each phrase for adequacy – how could any arrangement of words ever do? As much as anything that day, we wanted the words to say something on her behalf. Wanted them to express the triumph as well as the tragedy, the joy as well as the grief. What would she have wanted to leave us with? Not just her family but the hundred others who gathered there that day. Some sense of dignity, I know that, some sense of meaning. *The life I made*, she might have said, *was much more than the life that I lost.*

But as it turned out, none of us could say it, none of us could say anything, unable to trust ourselves to speak at all. Other people, friends, relatives, did it for us, and I was surprised by the comfort of it, by the words and the people overflowing the chapel, people who loved our mother, who loved us. I held myself upright among them until I heard someone helplessly sobbing – one of Ashley's teenaged boys. The sound undid me. One by one we folded then, everyone did, and the chapel filled with the soft noise of sorrow. It continued through the eulogy, until the song her sons had chosen sounded over our heads. 'Beautiful in My Eyes'. And the boys – all her sons and grandsons, Peter, Ashley, Andrew, John, Dane, Adrian, Kristian, Drew – carried her slowly, tenderly, out of the chapel and into the light.

★

No one noticed the grimace beneath Peter's tears. We were all too washed and buffeted by emotion. But as he shouldered his mother's coffin, a searing pain shot through his arms, back and legs. A small cost, and he would not speak of it, but a week later, his stoicism drained, his doctor will tell him his ankle is broken and has been for some time.

When it came time to divide up her things, we were generous with each other, scrupulously fair. We gathered at the house, reluctant, as if separating her possessions made her absence final. I listened to my sister and brothers and saw we were doing it the way she would have: *You have this / No, you take it, you haven't got one of those / You have that for Alyssa / Tamara should have this.* We spread things out on the bed and made even piles – rings and bracelets and earrings, books, pieces of clothing. Her sewing materials. Skeins of wool. A handwritten copy of the lyrics to 'The Rose'.

A week later, after Peter and Sharon had gone home, I sat at the table with my father and younger brothers. We'd sorted most of our mother's possessions, put things aside for her sisters, but there were still some precious items Dad hadn't been able to deal with. One in particular. *Who*, he said wearily over his unfinished coffee, *is going to get the painting?*

The painting is a pastel watercolour taken from the gypsy photograph of our mother. It's bigger than the photograph, the colours more muted, her expression not so nuanced. The artist has introduced, I think, a sweetness and contentment to my mother's face that dilutes the photo's pull, its suggestion of longing. It's a reinterpretation of the past, and we all look at it through the eyes of children who want to see their mother happy, a sweet smile on her lovely face. So we see what we want to see: a serene, beautiful creature who is also our mother. We glance at it as we pass, reassured that all is well.

We looked at each other, my brothers and I. Thinking the same thing. So it didn't matter who voiced it: *Peter*, someone said.

AFTERWORD

Four years after our mother died, in the middle of summer, Peter called me from Sydney. I was standing on a hot pavement in West End, juggling the phone and books I'd just bought at Avid Reader. At the other end, Peter was looking at his mail: a fat folder of papers, the official, government-stamped version of his childhood. He read aloud from some of the hospital and court documents and said, *You're the writer in the family. Why don't you write this story?* And he meant the tale of the polio survivor and the runaway this terrible paper trail represented, not the story of a child ripped from his mother. He didn't know that story himself.

So his question sounded simple, at first – and in many ways it was. Peter needed to make sense of it all, I thought, to make a recognisable shape for his life. His childhood was the stuff of myth, wild and insubstantial, hard to believe. He needed to make it all real – to pin it down by speaking it and seeing it written, by making it a *story*. One, perhaps, that he could believe too.

But as I listened to his accounts of the lock-ups, the privations, his life in the care of the State, I kept seeing the little boy looking for his mother, the face of the lost baby. *Peter*, I said finally, interrupting the sorrowful litany, *that's only part of it. The boy in the paperwork was stolen from his mother.* That's *his story.*

But that story wasn't simple at all, or straightforward in any way. Peter had spent most of his life creating a different one, a narrative in which he was the solitary protagonist, and it began not at his birth or his abduction but with polio. If its tragedies and sorrows were his alone, so were its ultimate triumphs – he was the self-made hero of his life, enduring his suffering, vanquishing his foes. There wasn't much choice: there had been no mother in that life, in reality or in the version he created. No mother, no earlier birth – this Peter was born with the calliper and the pain, already two years old. This was the Peter who had survived.

The boy stolen from his mother. The words had startled us both, made us hesitate. As if, along the telephone line between us, a shape had emerged suddenly out of silence. We had no way of knowing what the shape was, then. Peter said he'd think about the story; I told him I had to finish another book before I could. The truth was, we were both afraid. Peter of this new version of himself, and me of a new version of *myself*: one who would break the prohibitions and the secrecy of our lives, our mother's vetoes and bans. That was the shape in the silence.

The book I was writing then, the one I spoke of to Peter, was a novel about a woman who grieves for a lost child by burying her broken porcelain in the earth. My publisher chose for its cover an image of a china cup, fractured in three delicate pieces, and linked by the imprint of a single flower. The image is beautiful, tactile; it seems possible, when you touch the paper cover, to reach in and fit the pieces snugly together again.

This story, the one you have in your hands, is my family's broken cup. When I first began to write it, at a small pine table that once belonged to my parents, that's what I wanted to do: gather the scattered shards, glue them together with words and return the cup to my family, whole. I didn't want it for myself, then; didn't see what I'd inherited, how truly I was my mother's child. I was merely the teller of the tale, standing outside it, reporting what I found. That task alone looked big and frightening enough, mined with the usual traps of family stories – the reluctance of some to speak, the grip of promises, gaps in information, secrets. After decades of silence and subversion, even this act of straightforward storytelling seemed transgressive. The only safe way in was as a journalist, objective, writing in the third person. I'd been doing that for years.

But outcomes in writing are never neat or predictable, I should have known that. This is what happened: history, both personal and cultural, weighed in. Slowly, I began to see that the events that ruled my mother's life, though hidden to me, had also ruled mine. That I too was stuck, we all were stuck, at the instant Peter disappeared. We were born into the grief of it, the shock of it, and how could any of us have known? Even our mother hadn't known, as her arms emptied on that morning in 1950, that this moment was a fine sharp point on which all our lives would turn: hers, Peter's, my own father's, those of us yet unborn.

But the moment, I realised, did not belong to us alone. As I researched and wrote and queried and read, the extraordinary events that defined my family, making us singular, shuffled into place with events that defined a country, making us multiple, linked, emblematic. That moment on the train, our family's compass, itself turned on a larger pivot in Australian history: the wholesale abduction of children over centuries. We were just one family among many in a secretive culture, a compliant society, one that had witnessed and condoned the removal of children from their mothers – the illegitimate, the Indigenous, the poor – and remained silent.

My gradual understanding of all this was like a creature cracking open its own egg. Emerging to meaning, to the alarming clarity of who I was, what made me: this culture, this family, these ordinary people – or people struggling to be ordinary – the cascade of loss and grief through generations. The watermark left on each. Left on me, and passed by me to my children.

Peter sent me his files. If he'd wanted evidence for the rest of us of his life's tragedies, of his fortitude and suffering, and if he needed an explanation for the sourness that had enveloped his relationship with our mother in her final years, it was there in front of me then. Police reports, court transcripts, hospital records. Letters from social workers, doctors, psychiatrists, nurses, teachers. The casual dismissals, desertions, abandonment. The neglect of parent and State. And on every page the pale footprint of a boy, lost.

Why did no one intervene on Peter's behalf? The question rang in my head like a bleak refrain. How could this small, vulnerable boy be left to the savage mercies of bureaucracy, of individuals and institutions that glossed over his pain and his need, and allowed him to fall between the cracks of the police and welfare and medical systems that were allegedly there to protect him, to care for him?

There it was in the files: at every point where Peter and potential rescue intersected, someone failed him. It began on the train in Cairns, and continued through the next two decades. Peter was relegated to the margins of our general regard by youth, by disability, perhaps even by ethnicity, but certainly by the attitude that his life barely mattered, and that, at any rate, it was someone else's concern.

The answer was and still is difficult to comprehend, because these days, childhood is viewed by most as a hallowed time, and children are treasured. But it seemed to me that, sixty years ago, childhood was a euphemistic notion. We barely blinked as Aboriginal children were torn from their families. Or as babies born to unmarried women were forcibly taken and handed to others. Or as the children of the poor were carried off to orphanages and quaintly named 'homes' where they laboured for their benefactors in slave-like conditions, deprived of education, often of food, and almost universally of anything resembling love.

It's all recorded in commissions of inquiries and reports, in personal accounts both written and spoken, in radio and television and newspaper features, in novels and essays, photographs and songs, in speeches and plaques and statues. Chronicles of shame and commemoration. But evidence too that the children of certain groups were seen and treated as commodities, rather than a precious resource. How else could we all collude in their removal from their mothers? All children need their mothers. When we wrench them apart we set up myriad individual catastrophes, from which no one ever fully recovers.

The truth of this struck me like a blade when, not long after I received Peter's files, I was invited to work with some of the 'Forgotten Australians' who, as children, had been locked up and abused in institutions run by state and religious organisations. Another commission of inquiry had finished, and there was a thirst for the stories behind it to be written down. It took a long time for these people to trust me, a stranger from a relatively privileged background, to talk to me or to tell me about their lives. Some simply could not. There were no words for the pain and humiliation, the loss, the alienation. As children they'd been starved, thrashed, made to suffer freezing winters without clothes or shoes, made to work until their fingers bled. They were taunted, isolated, sexually, physically and emotionally abused. At night, they cried for their mothers.

Those who finally summoned the fortitude and guts to even try to articulate it took weeks, months, circling around their pasts as if, even now, the grief could explode and annihilate them. When they did speak I understood: these raw facts and memories could annihilate anybody. They all still lived in the skin of their younger selves, the past was still with them. Some of them simply could not and did not survive it.

These were the things that were happening to children in every part of the country, boys and girls, in the city and the bush, all through Peter's childhood years. No one tried to rescue them, either.

In the days after Peter had requested his records from government agencies in Sydney, the nightmares started. He didn't tell me about them for years, despite the hundreds of hours we'd spent together as I researched this book. It wasn't until recently, when I was struggling with the ending to his story, that something gave beneath the pressure of my questions.

He told me about the dreams in a telephone call. When they occurred, he said, he would wake in fright. Wet with sweat and pinned to the bed, uncertain if he was asleep or awake. He would try to move his limbs – right leg, left arm – but they were frozen. He said simply: 'It was terrifying.'

In another dream he was running, chased by enormous boulders. Thundering towards him, closer and closer, almost at his heels. Eventually, ragged with exhaustion, he reached a cliff, and jumped.

It didn't take him long to put things together: as he walked to get coffee after hours at home with his files, his sense of smell was heightened, and he would detect 'a particular body odour' when he walked past men in the street. That night, the nightmares would recur.

'That's when I began to face things,' he said. 'To face everything that had happened to me. It took years, because I had to re-live it all.' He paused, and I imagined him in the office of his unit in Newtown, his face to the window. 'The hardest thing was facing the reality of being molested, not just once but many times. The shame of it.'

It wasn't just within him: he had been made to feel ashamed at home after the first time, when Michael had been called in front of the judge. 'But it happened many times afterwards, especially on the streets when I was starving. I'll never forget that hunger. The men didn't pay me but they fed me. I hadn't realised how much shame I'd carried about it.'

But facing up to it in the years after his mother died was good for him, he said. 'I began to get it out of my system. I wish I'd done that before I'd even met Mum. I'd kept that anger and shame for years, and I was very good at denying. If I'd been the person I am now when I first met her, things would have been different.

'I know so much more now. That we were scared of each other. Looking back, I just wanted her to love me. That's what I felt that first night, when she looked at my tattoos and said, you wouldn't have had those if I had brought you up. Right then I realised she loved me, would have loved me.'

She was in Peter's files too, this mother whose love he craved. She is mentioned here and there, a woman who was either *deceased* or *ran away* from her son, but her shadow falls on Peter's footprints on each miserable page. As I read them I kept asking the question I'd begun with: how could a child be snatched from his mother, violently, in broad daylight, without anyone noticing or trying to help her? On the train and later – when she arrived in Brisbane, when she sought assistance in finding him and reclaiming him – why did no one intervene? That's what I wanted to know.

And of course, the answer was in the same places I'd found the answer about Peter – the inquiries and hearings and testimonies – because the destinies of mothers and children are always, in some way, entwined. At the time Peter was stolen, maternity and motherhood were euphemistic in the same way that childhood was. And if a child was removed from his or her mother, whether Aboriginal, illegitimate, poor or all three, then it was generally agreed it was *in the child's best interests.* In other words, the mother wasn't up to it, was bad or inept, not suitable, not good enough, *unentitled.* Someone else was entitled: someone white, someone married, someone rich.

It was part of the relegation of women at that time to the status of second-class citizen. The men were back from another war, from the immorality and outrage of mass killing, and women were easy receptacles for the anger and shame of it. In this newly puritan time, women were expected to uphold and embody a new moral universe: the chaste wife and mother behind the white picket fence, in the kitchen of a humble home. If the war still continued behind that fence, if there was anger and violence there, that was no one's business. A man's home was his castle. He'd fought for it, and it wouldn't be breached.

Of course, the issue was also about money, and fear, and class. If our mother had been rich, she might have engaged a powerful lawyer or a private investigator. She might have approached a society journalist, a friendly member of parliament. But her own background, her experience with Michael and the abuse she'd suffered, the shame she'd taken on, had erased any sense of entitlement she might have had to do anything. She was powerless.

One day in late autumn, some time after our conversation about his nightmares, I walked with Peter around the base of the massive pylons of the Sydney Harbour Bridge. He wanted to show me the places he'd slept rough as a child, the bushes and alcoves that sheltered him, the bins he ate from, the favourite haunts of the homeless men who shared their scraps with him. I squeezed between some low spreading branches on a slope overlooking the water, imagining myself in Peter's skin, dragging Peter's bad leg. Despite the startling view it was damp and exposed and alive with invisible creatures. Even the breeze off the harbour felt heartless. I was glad he hadn't taken Mum on this tour when she visited, and said so. Even if he did have things to prove to her, back then.

He laughed. *Maybe I did want to prove something back then*, he said. *That I was alright. But it wasn't conscious. I just had this burning question, and she was the answer to it.* He looked up at the scooped iron of the bridge. *But after she died, a real blackness descended. I felt desperate, knowing I hadn't been able to face it all. The truth. I was weak, a chicken shit.*

'When the painting arrived I hung it up and I'd stand in front of it and talk to her, and cry. Cry! I'd never cried in my life. I realised that meeting her had changed me.'

But it wasn't until he could interpret the events of his own life that he could begin to come to terms with how she'd changed him, and how much: the person he had been and the one she helped him become. Reading the documents, he said, helped him see that he'd been 'a victim'.

'You have to do that before you become a survivor,' he said. 'I had to come to terms with who I was, who I am, and stop trying to be someone else.' He smiled at me with that half-smile our mother had. 'I felt a bit sorry for myself then,' he said. 'I allowed myself a bit of empathy. And finally started to feel I was getting past it.'

I've found it hard to be still over the decade since my mother's death. I've moved house seven times, gone in and out of jobs. I've travelled the length and breadth of Australia, flown around the world: I met Lennart's children and visited his grave in Norway with my father; walked through Michael's village on Kythera with Sharon, and looked on as she met long-lost aunts and cousins in the taverna on the beach at Agia Pelagia. Wrote and walked in quiet villages in Yorkshire and in Wales. It's tempting to think it's been one long search, and sometimes, back in my writing room with silky oak and jacaranda flowering against the city skyline, I can imagine I've found its object, some slippery notion of myself that is nothing solid and nothing certain. But at least, perhaps, more than a filmy outline, more than a paper pattern.

After the days in Greece with Sharon, I came home to my desk and waited for the end of this book to announce itself. I had a sense of a circle turning, that I was moving towards its close, but my writer's eye kept straying to the beginning. If the circle was closing, it seemed important to know what it was closing *on*.

When summer arrived again I drove south along the coast for several hours to a beachside town to work without distraction. For a week I slept and worked in a small white room jutting out over rocks and sea. Each day I woke early to walk and swim before I settled at a round rattan table that was as different as it could be from my writing desk at home. The white wood of the windows framed a headland and a crescent of beach where dolphins came to play each afternoon. Below the balcony, the Pacific Ocean slumped and slapped across rocks cut and furred green by ageless tides. Seabirds wheeled and dived.

I worked to an uninterrupted rhythm, day and night, watching the movement of moon and sun over the crescent of beach. Was it this rhythm that allowed a shape to settle over the pages, fixing my thoughts and my pattern in place? I don't know. But as I trawled through notebooks and drafts in the warm salt air, I found this from my time in Yorkshire:

I'd like to think the pain meant something. I'd like to think some error or badness in me was being burned in its flames. That pain is a crucible. That it is something that merely wants to be understood.

I had to re-read it several times until I saw it: my whole family was in those sentences. My mother, Peter. I looked out at the ocean rising and falling and crashing below me. For so long I'd tried to run from my mother's history, so intent on differences I hadn't noticed the commonalities, not so much between mother and daughter but between woman and woman. I put down my pen. Looked out at the ocean rolling and breaking and retreating, re-making itself.

I cried for my mother then, not the dull self-pity I'd wept with after she died but a full and proper grief for what she had suffered. I felt that, for the first time, I knew something about the woman I was grieving. That, I saw, might be where the circle began and ended: in the writing of the story I had come back to her, and to myself.

There was still one thing left to do. I rang Peter in Sydney. *It wasn't fair*, I said as soon as he answered, and then stopped, unable to go on. *What's wrong?* Peter asked. I struggled for control of my voice; it felt important to say this. *We got the better deal, Pete. It was strange for us at times, but we had her, the best of her, and you missed out.* I was weeping again by then, barely able to spit out the words. But at the other end Peter laughed softly. *You did get the better deal,* he said. *But you know, it's okay. Better than okay – we were all lucky. That's what she taught us – to see the glass half-full.*

That evening, as the sky paled, I swam in the empty curve of beach below the headland. Immersed in the sea, in the sensation of yielding and rush, I thought again of Peter and the beach at Agia Pelagia where, years before, he'd swum out and away from the land, his body buoyed and powerful and full of joyous potential. I thought about acceptance and contentment. About luck and possibility: the ambition they find in us, to go out, out, towards unknown horizons, towards our real and better selves.

Yvonne at twenty-one

AUTHOR'S NOTE

How do you tabulate ten years in the life of a book, in the life of a writer, in the life of a family? By the losses and gains, arrivals and departures, by some vague quotient that measures what, who and how many? Time can be a sly trickster, colouring and confusing order and memory.

This is what happened as I sat down to write about the decade that has passed since this memoir was first published: the years and months, their orderly progression on the calendar, immediately began to warp. I thought it might be one of the lingering effects of the pandemic: not the disease itself, but the subliminal legacy of lockdown, the constant projections – backward and forward – to times before and those to come. I know I'm not alone in feeling a nostalgia, not just for the past but oddly for the future, a longing to return to the innocence that attended our days before 2019, and our fearless way of being in the world.

That might account partially for this struggle to set down the dates and events in some kind of order. How else to explain how I'd forgotten the year my son, Dane, and his family moved to the South Island of New Zealand? This was after the big Christchurch earthquakes; their decision had felt like a quake in our hearts. I remember them leaving, waving from the departure gate, the children clinging to their parents' hips. The tears that wouldn't stop as I drove home through streets that looked empty of joy. Still, I had to call Dane for confirmation: was it before or after *Boy, Lost* was published in early 2013? *The year before, Mum*, he said, laughing.

And there was more: when had Zoe, my daughter, moved back to Brisbane from Sydney, where she'd been studying acting at NIDA? And was it 2016 or 2017 when I'd walked across England, from west to east, celebrating the completion of a novel, testing myself? There's a photograph on the wall: I'm at Robin Hood's Bay in North Yorkshire, about to hurl a pebble I'd picked up at the start of my walk at St Bees in Cumbria. It's a ritual. When was it?

Beneath this barrage of uncertainty, I've raged against the disappearance of traditional photographs and the albums that once forced a lazy kind of chronology on our lives and our memories. We could go to them to immediately re-enact a certain time or era, to look for answers or clarification or clues. The order and arrangement of pictures in an album gave us a context and a narrative; they leant coherence to times we had lived. That's what I needed: the carefully placed pictures that gave not just a chronology, but clues to who we were then.

A mobile phone is a clever machine, but as an archive it often fails me. The photographs it produces and stores feel ephemeral, easily killed off with a swipe or a tap. And they're often out of their original context, easily manipulated, easily erased. On the other hand, it takes an act of will to destroy a paper photograph. The act of ripping or cutting implies violence, something broken – a family, a relationship, a heart.

But there it is: for the past decade, I must rely on digital images of my family, retrieved from various phones. From memory and the emotions that attend them I begin to piece together certain events, beginning with the launch of *Boy, Lost* at an overcrowded café in Highgate Hill, Brisbane. It was a year of reckoning. Our father, Kjell-Arne, a hero in our family story, had begun to fail the year before. But here he is at the launch, smiling and laughing, and as always keen to go home.

Zoe was with him, holding newly born Oskar B Kjell, the miracle baby she never thought she'd have, and named for her grandfather. And here are Peter and Sharon, virtual carbon copies of each other, smiling and laughing together. My younger brothers and their families. My mother's sister, Evelyn, and her Edward, our Uncle Ted. But of course there's a hole in the picture: Dane is missing. He was already in New Zealand.

Later in 2013, more holes opened up in our hearts and lives. The deepest one held our father. He died peacefully in September that year. He had remarried some years after our mother's death, on his eightieth birthday – Evy, a childhood friend, had moved from Sweden to be with him. They had nine good years together. I suppose we thought they'd have nine more.

We loved Evy. Afterwards, we watched as she struggled to decide: to stay in this warm place with people she'd come to love, or to return home to her son and granddaughter? In the end, Sweden won. Within a year, there was another gap in our lives.

Time stretches, but it also mends us. In the same year our father died, Peter became a grandfather. His daughter, Tamara, married, and the arrival of her children, Oliver, and later, Sienna, brought him extraordinary happiness. The dates should be imprinted on my brain. But once more, I had to consult Peter. He had no trouble, of course, remembering the year – *the miracle*, he called it – when he became not just Peter, but *Grandad*.

There were milestones for Sharon too. Some years earlier, we'd met up in Athens and flown together to Kythera, the island birthplace of her biological father, Michael. It was important for both of us. It would be Sharon's first meeting with her Greek aunts and uncles and cousins, and a chance to come to some kind of understanding of Michael and his terrible cruelty to our mother.

Sharon returned to Kythera in 2016 – I've checked the dates – with her son and his family, to meet the relatives they scarcely knew they had. And again in 2018. (Covid prevented another planned visit in 2020.) For Sharon, these visits are important. Kjell-Arne will forever be her father, and we her siblings, but her devotion to her Greek family, her constancy, has cemented her place in a bloodline with people who love her and claim her as their own.

Peter hasn't returned to the island since his trip there as a much younger man. Polio, we've all realised, never really goes away. Its effects move through Peter's body with the years, restricting his mobility, thinning his bones. He is, we've learned – we have to drag it out of him – in constant pain. He once memorably said to our mother: *I don't let it stop me.* And now, these years on, he doesn't. He is an active member of his community, has a weekly date with his grandchildren, is well-known around Newtown and, until the pandemic, made regular trips to Brisbane.

Boy, Lost, all five or six years of researching and writing it, and the years of touring, gave Peter and I a whole new relationship. I stayed so often with him in his small apartment that the second bedroom has become mine. Peter's official files were hard to read, his memories hard to hear, but his enormous inner strength, his resilience and generosity, came shining through.

These days it's more difficult for him to travel. A couple of falls have badly affected his weak leg and landed him in hospital. He's more cautious now.

Some years before my father died, I'd taken him to the north of Norway, to see two granddaughters he'd never met. His son, Lennart, had died in the same year as my mother, and though my father grieved him he was in no shape to travel the arc of the earth for another funeral. But two years later, we did. We flew first to Oslo, where we stayed with friends – three sisters, living on their father's pine farm – then took two flights, a bus and a ferry to Dønna. The scenes as we disembarked, my father searching faces for one like his son's, will never leave me.

I went back to the island – just south of the Lofotens – after *Boy, Lost* was published. But memory is suspect here too. Was it before or after our father died? It can only, I think, have been afterwards. This time I drove with my cousin, Jan-Ake, from the south of Sweden and up through the glassmaking province, which inspired a novel, *Shell*. Then over the mountains into Norway. Far into the Norwegian summer night, when the soft lemon light never really darkens, we spoke about Lennart, about Kjell Arne. About the ties of blood and their mysteries.

This conversation came back to me in New Zealand. I can't ever forget the moment, nor the year: 2018. In the bar at Christchurch Airport, my son told me about a young woman who'd contacted him, looking for her father, hoping he might be able to help. I was distracted, itching to see my grandchildren. *And did you*, I asked, playing with the tag on my suitcase, *help her find her dad?* In Dane's face, a range of possibilities between heartbreak and joy. *Yes*, he said finally. I *had a DNA test and it came back positive.* He had my attention now. These are the things he tells me: he was sixteen. A long-ago Saturday afternoon, a girl he had worked with. He barely remembered the day. He didn't think of possibilities. They parted not knowing their future had already begun.

Her name is Tahlia, he said, smiling a boy's smile. And then we both began to cry.

We drove home with snow-capped mountains in our view, talking and weighing this confounding new reality, the newness and joy. But in the silences, one thing was implicit: the fugitive outline of missing children. It was as if my son had stepped into a stencil, one that had shaped my family for generations. The cascade of loss and grief. The watermark left on each generation.

He turned to me and said: *I've missed out on her. Twenty-one years of her. It doesn't seem fair.*

But perhaps the watermark stops here. Perhaps there is a way to claw back what was lost. Months later, in Brisbane, there was my son, coming up the stairs, behind a young woman with eyes I already knew. Impossible, of course; I'd never seen her before. Not even a photograph. But: *you are one of mine*, I thought as she stepped over the threshold. My son smiled a shy smile. *This is your granddaughter,* he said. I opened my arms. To imprint every feature – shoulders and back, hands, cheekbones. As if she had just been born.

Now, I watch Tahlia with her siblings, with Ben, her staunch ally, and with their own baby son. I think of her courage, her openness, her capacity for acceptance and joy. And dare to hope we might be freed from the terror of loss. That we might claw back, after all, what we missed.

—Kristina Olsson, Brisbane, 2023

ACKNOWLEDGMENTS

A book is rarely written in isolation. This one has been nurtured by many hearts and hands. So many people have contributed stories, memories, anecdotes, snatches of history, and this book navigates them all. I have tried to respect each version of the truth, but this story represents my own, and I take full responsibility for it. My deepest gratitude goes to my family, who have borne the intrusions of questions with grace and humility: my father, my sister and brothers and sisters-in-law, my aunts, my children. To my mother, whose story I inherited, and whose abiding goodness and sense of honour I can only hope to emulate. And to Evy, who married my father on his eightieth birthday and whose very presence in all our lives has been a blessing.

I have also had the great fortune of the friendship of extraordinary women, who have all in some way sustained me over the years of writing this book. In no particular order, I thank Marg, Jill, Sandra, Mary-Rose, Sarah, Nike, Anna, Donna, Sue, Emma, Andrea, Debbie, Emma, Jane, Sally, Rosie, Jo, Krissy, Allison, Anne, Janine, Mary, Juls, and my beloved writers group members – Fred, Toska, Alex and Sarah.

I acknowledge the support of the Literature Board of the Australia Council for a New Work grant to complete this work; Varuna, The Writers' House, for a residential fellowship; Arts Queensland, and tutors and fellow writers at the Arvon Foundation's Lumb Bank in Yorkshire.

Fiona Inglis, Madonna Duffy and Judith Lukin-Amundsen: all much more to me than agent, publisher, editor.

And finally, my children, Zoe and Dane, and their partners, Tamsin and Anita: what can I say? Your love and support is the whole world. And of course, Amber, Axel, and the one we call Pelé: you have my heart.